Community Care
Practice Handbooks

General Editor: Martin Davies

Groupwork

7

Community Care
Practice Handbooks

General Editor: Martin Davies

Groupwork

Allan Brown

COMMUNITY
CARE

Gower

First published in hardback 1986 by
Gower Publishing Company Limited

This paperback edition published 1989 by
Wildwood House Limited
Gower House,
Croft Road,
Aldershot,
Hampshire GU11 3HR,
England

Gower Publishing Company
Old Post Road,
Brookfield,
Vermont 05036,
USA

British Library Cataloguing in Publication Data

Brown, Allan
  Groupwork. - 2nd ed. - (Community care practice handbooks;
  2)
  1.Social group work
  1.Title   II.Series
  361.4   HV45

Library of Congress Cataloging-in-Publication Data

Brown, Allan G.
  Groupwork.
  (Community care practice handbooks; 2)
  Bibliography :p.
  Includes index.
  1 Social group work - Great Britain. I. Title.
II. Series.[DNLM: 1.Group Processes. 2 Social Work. HV 45 B877g]
HV45.B74 1986   361.4'0941   86-12037

ISBN 0 7045 0633 5

Set by Action Typesetting Limited, Gloucester
Printed and bound in Great Britain by Biddles Ltd, Guildford,
Surrey.

Contents

Acknowledgements

1st edition

I am indebted to numerous people who have shared with me their groupwork experience, feelings and ideas. They include many group members, social work students and teachers, social workers and probation officers in Britain and in Michigan, USA. In particular, Frank Maple of the University of Michigan and Nano McCaughan, recently of the National Institute of Social Work, London, have stimulated and encouraged me in my interest in groupwork.

I would like to thank Christine Stones, Derek Lockhart, Phyllida Parsloe and Brian Caddick (of Bristol University) for reading draft chapters and offering support and critical comment.

I am grateful to Margaret Harris and Georgina Coleman for typing drafts, and to Pam Gallagher for typing the final manuscript. It is doubtful whether I could ever have completed the task without the loving support of my wife, Celia, who has given me encouragement when I most needed it.

2nd edition

I am again indebted to the many people from whom I have continued to learn about groupwork. A special thanks this time to Carol Keen for typing all the revised parts of the manuscript so helpfully and efficiently.

Introduction to the Second Edition

I have been very surprised and very delighted at the positive reception given to this book by practitioners, students and trainers since it was first published in 1979. I have not, therefore, made any major changes to the basic format of the book, but there are two main reasons for producing this new edition. The first is to bring the book up to date with the developments in groupwork in the 1980s by guiding the reader to important new publications and practice developments which have contributed to our growing understanding of the knowledge and skills needed by groupworkers. The American-based quarterly journal, *Social Work with Groups* (Haworth Press) has transformed the quality and range of groupwork literature available, and it is frequently referenced in this text. The British literature continues to expand gradually, with a few new books (e.g. Heap, 1985; Whitaker, 1985), accounts of groupwork practice spread around different journals, and still much important innovative work going unrecorded. I hope that before the third edition of this book is published (!) British/European groupworkers will have their own specialist journal.

The second reason for producing this new edition has been the opportunity to re-write some sections of the book, to share developments in my own and colleagues' understanding of groupwork practice. These sections include those on groupwork aims and models (Chapter 1), group composition and groupwork planning (Chapter 2), co-leadership (Chapter 3), difficulties which arise in groups and possible ways of resolving them (Chapter 4), and groupwork consultation and evaluation (Chapter 5). Many more specific developments are alluded to and referenced, e.g. working with groups in residential and day-care settings, the significance of race and gender in groupwork, the special skills needed for pre-group meetings and open groups, but limitations on space in an introductory text precludes the detailed consideration which each of these merits.

1. Groupwork in Social Work

Background developments in groupwork

Groupwork in Britain has come a long way since the 1960s when it was a relatively scarce commodity. It was rarely included in social work training courses, carried an unhelpful mystique associated with sensitivity and encounter groups, and was often regarded as an idiosyncratic activity in those agencies where it was practised by innovative social workers. The available literature was North American. In the USA at that time groupwork was already well established as a social work method, going through a phase of being separated off as a distinct specialism (this changed subsequently in North America in the 1970s when groupwork became re-integrated with mainstream practice, and it has moved forward with a whole new vigour and impetus since 1978 when the groupwork journal was launched, and since when large-scale annual groupwork symposia have been held).

The 1970s saw groupwork gradually being taken more seriously in the UK, perhaps partly due to the North American influence, but more likely due to the push for diversification and improvement of practice intervention methods arising in part from discouraging research evaluations of the efficacy of traditional one-to-one casework methods. A number of British introductory groupwork texts were published in the period 1975–80 (Davies, 1975; Douglas, 1976; Douglas, 1978a; Heap, 1979; McCaughan, 1978) offering a firmer basis for groupwork learning during training, and for groupwork practice in agencies. There was increasing evidence (see Stevenson/Parsloe, 1978) from social workers of a widespread wish to use groupwork methods being tempered by a lack of encouragement (if not active opposition) in some social work agencies. By contrast, some Social Services Departments appointed specialist groupwork consultants and this type of commitment has often been reflected in the extent and quality of groupwork practice in that agency (see Laming and Sturton, 1978; McCaughan, 1985). In many Probation Areas, groupwork has achieved recognition as a mainstream method of working, both at intake (see Brown and Seymour, 1983) and in a whole range of groups which are offered. Statutory recognition and the specific allocation of considerable resources have led to intermediate treatment groupwork (Jones and Kerslake, 1979) being uniquely supported in statutory agencies. Another development in the 1980s, spearheaded by voluntary agencies, is the establishment of family-centres and a whole range of day-care and short-term residential care provision, offering enormous scope for working with people in groups and groupings, both formal and informal.

Groupwork in the UK in the 1980s is struggling to develop new levels of coherence and sophistication, as interest shifts from the basics of groupwork to the specific knowledge and skills needed for particular kinds of groups in particular kinds of contexts, using specific types of methods. As I write this (early 1986), there are signs of moves towards a stronger identity for groupwork and groupworkers as national and local networks get established, different groupwork approaches are debated in the journals, and ways of launching a specialist groupwork journal are being actively explored.

The research-based case for groupwork is no more proven, but certainly no less so, than that for casework. Because of the complexity of researching groupwork practice, and of mounting comparative studies, it will be a long time before worthwhile research evidence becomes available. Even then, it will only be meaningful at a level of sophistication which discriminates between different methods of groupwork, matched to particular needs, user groups and objectives. Meanwhile, those of us who are committed to the development of groupwork as a method to stand on equal terms with other methods have to base our commitment mainly on subjective criteria, experience and value-judgements.

I know personally that *some* groups can be a very effective method of helping *some* individuals, because I have experienced this potency at first hand. As a group member, I have been helped with my own painful and difficult personal problems on several occasions. I have led or co-led groups in which I have witnessed the efficacy of the group as a context in which people can help each other, develop skills and solve problems. Follow-up studies and consumer feedback confirm this at a subjective level, as do journal articles which attempt to evaluate a particular group's 'success'. (Those which 'fail' are rarely written about, but can be equally illuminating!) There are also some basic therapeutic and learning processes such as peer-support, mutual helping, role-modelling and feedback which are uniquely characteristic of the group setting.

As stated in the first edition of this book, I do not see groupwork as a social work panacea, and the following pages indicate both its potential and its hazards. What I hope the book will continue to achieve is a demystification of groupwork as a method of intervention. It will be shown that groupwork is an umbrella term for a wide range of activities and therapies, and that there are certain basic concepts and skills which can be relatively easily acquired by the practitioner who wishes to extend her* repertoire of creative response to complex human need.

What is groupwork?

Most books on groupwork begin with a detailed analysis of definitions, firstly of the term 'small group' and then of the term 'groupwork'. For the purpose of this book we shall assume that readers share some common notion of what a small group is, but that there is more confusion about what is meant by groupwork. We shall therefore dispose rapidly of the former by taking E. J. Thomas's (1967) working definition of a small group as 'a collection of individuals who are interdependent with one another and who share some conception of being a unit distinguishable from other collections of individuals'. This covers the key concepts of *a defined membership, interdependence* and *boundary* ('distinguishable' implies some boundary). We need to add the *size* of the collection of individuals, which would normally be thought of as in the range 3–14 persons, and the notion that small groups exist for some *purpose*, however ill-defined.

Before defining groupwork, it is useful to be aware of the range of groups with which social workers may be involved. These can be represented diagrammatically by 7 circles (see Fig. 1.1, page 4).

The three cirlces (1–3) above the horizontal line refer to the range of groups with which this book is most directly concerned. They are groups in which the social worker is working directly with clients/group members, and in some acknowledged leadership or resource

---

*The female gender is used throughout this book as a shorthand reference to social workers of both sexes, and, similarly, the male gender is used for group members. In group examples and illustrations the gender chosen is appropriate to the context. The terms social worker, groupworker and practitioner are used interchangeably. 'Groupworker' refers to a social worker when she is practising groupwork and is not intended to refer to groupwork specialists of whom there are very few in the UK.

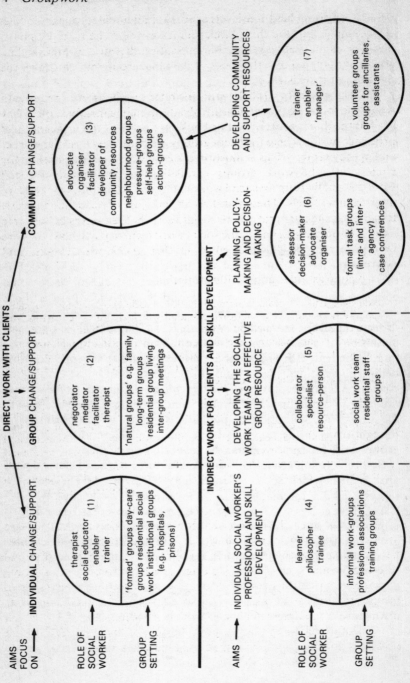

Fig. 1.1 Groups in social work differentiated by aims, the role of

role. Every group has three levels of focus: individual, group and social environment, but the three circles indicate where the main emphasis lies. This is inevitably an over-simplification, because as McCaughan (1978) has pointed out, the focus of the same group may shift over the duration of its existence.

The four circles (4−7) below the line refer to other work groups with which the social worker may be involved, often in a member role. They are not the direct concern of this book, but some of the principles and processes outlined here for client groups are paralleled in social worker and agency groups. This is illustrated by the vertical positioning of the circles with the work groups paralleling the individual (= social worker), small group (= social work team) and community (= agency/inter-agency) levels. These parallels are not just of academic interest. Experience suggests that where social workers themselves collaborate effectively in groups, and in the social work team in particular, they are more likely to be group-oriented in their work with clients, and conversely.

Two contrasting examples illustrate this.

Example: This is a team in name only. Each social worker functions quite separately, protective of her own caseload which she rarely discusses with team colleagues. Her method of working is based on individual and family casework. Team meetings are infrequent and restricted to administrative matters. There is no groupwork and an attempt by two trainees to introduce it is unsuccessful because a group-oriented culture which includes sharing clients is alien to the prevailing ethos.

Example: This team has had the same membership for two years. Over this period a culture of sharing and mutual trust has been developed. Team meetings are frequent and include sharing of work problems, mutual evaluation and feedback, and creative discussion of new developments and ways of working. Groupwork of several kinds, intermediate treatment groups, family therapy and various community projects are integral parts of the team programme. The social workers often work in pairs and sometimes three or four are involved in different roles with members of the same family.

The reader may like to consider how many of these seven types of groups she is currently involved with, and in what roles. Also relevant is her 'invisible' eighth circle which represents the internalised personal reference groups such as family of origin, peer and social groups. These personal groups influence the roles taken and the feelings experienced in group situations at work. The term 'client' or group member does not distinguish a separate category of persons, but indicates a role which any one of us may take at any time. 'The doer of the Golden Rule, and he who is done by, is the same man, *is* man.' (Erikson)

Definitions of groupwork

One of the most useful definitions of groupwork against which to set the discussion so far is that developed by Konopka (1963): 'Social group-work is a method of social work which helps individuals to enhance their social functioning through purposeful group experiences, and to cope more effectively with their personal, group or community problems.'

This definition makes a number of basic points: groupwork is a method of social work: it helps individuals with their social functioning; it is purposeful; and it is concerned with coping at personal, group and community levels.

The emphasis is, however, rather the traditional one of helping the individual with a problem. Contemporary groupwork emphasises action and influence as well as reaction and adaptation. The definition becomes more comprehensive if we add: groupwork provides a context in which *individuals help each other*; it is a method of *helping groups* as well as helping individuals; and it can enable individuals and groups to *influence* and *change* personal, group, organisational and community problems.

There are several difficulties about defining the boundaries of what we call 'groupwork'. The term 'social groupwork' is used by Konopka and others to describe groupwork with an emphasis on *social function-ing*, and to distinguish it from *group therapy*, where the emphasis is on emotional needs and psychological processes. Psychotherapeutic groups are included in this text under the term 'groupwork' because there are many similarities with other forms of groupwork and many social workers work with this type of group. Another boundary problem arises over family therapy—work with the family as a group—because this archetypal 'natural' group has much in common with other kinds of social work groups, but also much that is unique. Family therapy is excluded here because it is a social work method in its own right, and the reader is referred to introductory books by Gorrell-Barnes (1984) and Treacher and Carpenter (1984).

Perhaps the most difficult boundary to define is that within the over-lap area between groupwork and community work. Social work with community groups can be regarded as a form of groupwork when the groups are relatively small, the aims local and neighbourhood-centred, as in community social work, and when the methods include giving some attention to group interaction and process.

Lastly, training and support groups for volunteers (see Fig. 1.1) and student supervision groups have much in common with some forms of direct groupwork with clients.

The practice guidelines in this book are intended to apply to a wide range of groups, but the emphasis will tend to be on *formed groups*, that is groups which have been specially composed for some purpose. This is because the author's own experience has been mostly in this area, and many of the groups with which social workers are concerned *are* specially formed ones. [There is good coverage of some specialised aspects in other texts, e.g. on family therapy, intermediate treatment, and community groups.] A full range of settings is included, taking in statutory and voluntary agencies, and institutional (e.g. prisons, hospitals), residential social work, day-care and community-based contexts.

Aims of groupwork

The aims of groupwork are many, but before attempting any classification, there are two important questions which should be considered. Firstly, *whose aims are they*? The agency, the social worker, the group members and the community will all have different perspectives on what the same group is for. (An example is given in Chapter 2.) Secondly, *how explicit are the aims*? Are they overt (disclosed), covert (known, but not disclosed) or unconscious (not known at the time)? One reason for trying to be clear about aims in any group is to minimise the 'hidden agenda'.

One of the best-known classifications of groupwork models, by aims, is that by Papell and Rothman (1966). They distinguish the *remedial, reciprocal* and *social goals* models, whose aims are respectively individual social adaptation, mediation between individuals and society (those social agencies which impinge on them directly) and increased social justice. These three aims correspond quite closely to the three levels of focus identified in Fig. 1.1. Each also indicates its own value emphasis.

> *Example*: A group for parents of children 'at risk'. With a 'remedial' focus, the aim might be to help the parents change their ways of treating their children. With a 'reciprocal' focus the aim could be to see how the parents and the groupworker might influence the child welfare agency to provide day-care facilities, and how the parents with help might organise themselves into a mutual support system to be called on as a safety-valve at times of stress. With a 'social goals' focus the aim might be improved social and housing conditions for underprivileged families in the area.

The Papell and Rothman categories are not specific enough for practice purposes, and a more detailed classification of aims is needed. The following is suggested, working from the individual to the societal levels, and bearing in mind that some categories may often overlap and be combined.

(a) *Individual assessment*. These groups are primarily for the assessment of individual needs/abilities/behaviour. The assessment data comes from a combination of self-assessment, worker-assessment and peer-assessment, the latter being the essential group ingredient. Such groups may be used with, for instance, prospective foster-parents; adult or juvenile offenders; new admissions to, or prospective discharges from, residential establishments.

(b) *Individual support and maintenance*. These are groups designed primarily to support individuals facing difficult personal or social circumstances. They include groups for people with a disability themselves, e.g. mentally handicapped adolescents, and groups for those who care for them, e.g. their parents (who are in what Whitaker, 1985, p.75, calls a 'linked-fate' relationship). Sometimes external aims emerge, e.g. to obtain better day-care facilities for the handicapped adolescents.

(c) *Individual change*. This large category includes different (and overlapping) kinds of individual change, ranging from specific behaviours to personal development:
— *social control* e.g. a group to help sex-offenders avoid re-offending
— *socialisation* e.g. a group to enable institutionalised people to learn social skills
— *interpersonal behaviour* e.g. assertiveness training groups
— *personal attitudes and values* e.g. a group for drug addicts to influence attitudes to 'pushing'
— *material circumstances* e.g. a group for unemployed men seeking work
— *self-concept and feelings* e.g. a group to raise the self-esteem of oppressed minorities
— *personal growth and development* e.g. an encounter group or 'T' group

(d) *Educational, information-giving and training*. e.g. groups on welfare rights, parenting, health education, volunteering.

(e) *Leisure/compensatory*. The aim of these groups is to provide individuals with leisure pursuits/enjoyable experiences to compensate for lacks in their personal lives.

(f) *Mediation between individuals and social systems*. These groups involve reciprocal transactions between individuals and social agencies, with change expected 'on both sides', e.g. a psychiatric hospital discharge group in which the social worker mediates between patients and the hospital authorities to facilitate the return to outside living.

(g) *Group change and/or support*. These are mostly natural or existing groups where the aims are primarily at the group level, e.g. a family group to improve family communication; work with a delinquent gang to divert their energies into more acceptable activities, a residential group to improve the quality of group living.

(h) *Environmental change*. This type of group attempts to influence the members' social environment, e.g. a residents' group to develop leisure facilities or oppose a road development; a single parents' group to press for day-care facilities for the children of working parents.

(i) *Social change*. These groups aim at social and political change, raising individual consciousness and redistributing power from institutional systems, e.g. local government, to the people. This is a controversial aim in a statutory agency and it falls outside some people's definition of groupwork. Like its polar opposite, social control of individual behaviour, it has political purposes and values.

In terms of the Papell and Rothman classification, the aims of category (c) are broadly remedial, (f) and (g) emphasise reciprocity, and (h) and (i) are concerned with social goals. Whether groups in categories (d) and (e) are social groupwork or are simply groupings of people learning/playing together, will depend on whether the group process is consciously regarded as a significant and important part of what happens.

Heap (1977) has suggested six principal aims of groupwork: alleviating isolation; promoting social learning and maturation; preparing for an approaching crisis or other life change; solving or clarifying problems at the person/familial level; solving or clarifying problems in the members' environment; achieving insight.

Why and when groupwork?

Some of the aims of groupwork, particularly those concerned with individual change and support, could be (and mostly are) pursued at the casework level. What is the distinctive feature of a group approach, and what are its potential advantages and disadvantages compared with other approaches?

There are some agencies in Britain, and many in the USA, which offer a range of alternative methods, and the client can choose which to opt for, or take more than one in combination. Even when choice is offered, the intake social worker has some responsibility to advise and give information to facilitate the choice. What evidence and knowledge is available to guide these decisions and choices?

Research findings from social psychology (e.g. M. Sherif and C.W. Sherif, 1969) clearly indicate that under certain conditions individual behaviour and attitudes are influenced by groups. This information is consistent with ordinary life experience of group-membership but it does not necessarily follow that groups created or assisted by social workers are successful in achieving their aims. Direct evidence about the efficacy of groupwork in relation to other methods or non-intervention is sparse and inconclusive, drawing on a few studies, mainly in the psychiatric setting, and all bedevilled by methodological problems. McCaughan (1978) was unable to include in her reader a chapter on research into groupwork outcome because of the shortage of material. She mentioned a few studies (e.g. The Wincroft Project, Smith *et al.*, 1972) as 'some positive evidence for the effectiveness of groupwork', and others can be found scattered around the literature (Glasser, Sarri and Vinter, 1974, Chapters 20–29). Studies (Parloff and Dies, 1977) in the psychiatric field give some indication that a combined individual and group approach may be more effective for some 'patients' than either method alone. The following guidelines are based on general information about groups, practice experience and subjective evaluation.

Some potential advantages of the groupwork method

Much social living is experienced in groups. This is apparent in the family, at work and in leisure activities. A natural group *is* real life, and a created group provides a setting where problems of interpersonal relationships and social skills can be worked on at first hand. The skills can then be transferred to natural settings.

Groups of people with similar needs can be a source of mutual support, mutual aid and problem solving. People in painful and difficult situations, e.g. spouses of stroke patients, sex offenders, or parents of autistic children, often feel completely alone and different. A social worker can reassure an individual that many others feel like him and know just what it's like, but when this is experienced directly in a group of similarly placed people it carries conviction. There is the relief of discovering that one's feelings are 'normal', and the example and advice of others about how to cope.

Attitudes, feelings and behaviour may be changed in a group situation. This can occur through *social interaction*, including *role-modelling, reinforcement, feedback* and the range of ideas available to each member.

> *Example*: An alcoholic, teetering on the brink of attempting sobriety, meets in an AA group other alcoholics who have been where she has been, who know the hell and the conflict which she is experiencing, and are now recovered and leading fulfilling lives.

> *Example*: The lone father, whose wife left him 3 months ago, and who feels depressed and desperate, meets other lone fathers who have been separated longer and have developed new life-styles and ways of coping. They are a living proof that change is possible for him too.

In these examples group members role-model personal change and problem solving, reinforce each other by mutual support and positive feedback, and extend the range of possibilities by sharing different ideas and ways of coping. A prerequisite for change is therapeutic optimism, a belief that change is possible and that there is hope. A group can provide this kind of climate, which can be used constructively or destructively.

In a group, every member is a potential helper. The roles of social worker and client are much less differentiated in a group, because much of the helping and the leadership comes from members of the group and the social worker is more exposed as a person. Groups can reveal hidden strengths and potential in individuals who have become habituated to labels such as 'useless' and 'inadequate'.

A group can be democratic and self-determining, giving more power to the 'client'. This is the political corollary of mutual helping. Unlike a one-to-one interview, a client in a group has numerical compensation for his weaker role-position. If there is consensus among group members they are in a powerful position to influence the social worker and the agency. This is one of the reasons why groupwork is viewed with apprehension by some social workers and some agencies. It is a major attraction for those who favour a more participatory, activist model of social work intervention.

A group setting is particularly suitable for some clients. There are some people who find the intensity and intimacy of a one-to-one relationship very difficult to cope with, and are much more comfortable in a group of peers. This is true for many adolescents who feel threatened by individual encounters with adults in authority.

Groupwork may be more economical of social worker time and effort. This is a frequently used argument of doubtful validity, especially in formed groups where the social worker is involved in all the preparatory work creating the conditions for the group to take place. In residential and day-care settings, where group members are physically available, there may be economies of time and effort, depending on how much energy is consumed maintaining space for the group in the larger institution.

Some potential disadvantages of the groupwork method

Confidentiality is more difficult to maintain than in one-to-one work. In a group, by definition, you share yourself and information about you with more people, and the risk of confidentiality being breached is that much greater, particularly as most of the people are not bound by a professional ethic. Some group agreement about confidentiality can reduce but not remove the risk. (Confidentiality is discussed in more detail in the section on values and ethics, p. 24.)

'Formed' groups are complex to plan, organise and implement. The work involved in preparing this type of group is considerable, and there are often obstacles to overcome at client, colleague and agency levels.

Groups require resources. The social worker is likely to be involved in negotiations for accommodation, transport, equipment and funds.

The individual gets less exclusive attention in a group. Some individuals, at least at some stages of their development, cannot cope with the sharing and competition involved in a group setting, and need the exclusive attention of an individual relationship. In a group they may be very disruptive, passive, hurt or scapegoated. Sometimes a period of individual work can be a preparation for group participation.

Group membership can increase labelling and stigma. Certain types of group sometimes attract labels, e.g. single-parents group, school-refusers group, sex-offenders group, alcoholics group, schizophrenics group, prisoners' wives group. Some people's primary need is 'normalisation' and the last thing they want is a group identity reinforcing their stigmatised label. The name of a group needs careful thought, and neutral titles such as 'Wednesday group' can reduce the danger of stigma.

Groups may be damaging for a small minority. This is not so much a disadvantage of groupwork as a reason for protecting people from being placed in unsuitable groups, and for selecting group leaders carefully. Lieberman, Yalom and Miles (1973) and Galinsky and Schopler (1977) have both produced some evidence that some people can be damaged in experiential groups. Their findings are discussed in the section on values and ethics (p. 26.).

Groupwork or family therapy?

There are, of course, other alternatives to groupwork besides one-to-one casework, notably work with couples and family therapy. In some situations family therapy is not practicable, either because the 'client' is not a member of an available family, or the family is not prepared to approach problems on a group basis. But there will be many cases where there is a genuine choice to be made by the social worker *and* the client(s) between the two methods.

So far as this writer is aware, no clear differential criteria have been established by family therapy and groupwork practitioners. One indicator is the extent to which the problem of an individual appears to be symptomatic of dysfunction in the whole family as a system, and the extent to which it is idiosyncratic to the individual and/or related to other systems such as school, work, and peer groups. One of the few published attempts to make a comparative study (Roman, 1976) indicates that choices tend to be made on the basis of the practitioner's personal philosophy and conceptual framework (focused around the primacy or otherwise of the family group) rather than on any established criteria.

One interesting development is couples groups in which several couples facing similar difficulties meet together as a group, thus combining features of both methods. Selection of methods needs careful consideration, and they may be effective in combination, e.g. an ex-psychiatric hospital patient may have family therapy for working at family adjustments on his return, and also attend a social skills group to develop his ability to cope in the community. Alternatively, if he has no family, he may need individual support sessions to gain the confidence to join a group.

What is it like being a social worker doing groupwork?

There are some special features of groupwork which will affect those social workers who practice it.

(*a*) A high level of commitment is necessary for the social worker who is leader or co-leader. It is relatively easy (though not necessarily desirable!) to postpone a commitment with one individual or even a family, but what if a group of ten are expecting you on an off day?

(*b*) Much effort and careful thought needs to go into planning.

(*c*) Groupwork is *pro-active*, in the sense that a positive professional initiative is usually involved, i.e. groupwork does not just happen, as casework can, it has to be initiated.

(*d*) Groupwork is more visible to others than one-to-one work, and tends to attract proportionately more attention in the agency. This sometimes results in higher expectations of 'success' than those applied to less visible individual work.

(*e*) Groupwork tends to arouse more anxiety in the worker and the agency. The notion of having to obtain permission tends to apply more.

(*f*) Groupwork involves sharing, both by clients and by social workers and their colleagues.

(*g*) Groupwork often highlights technical and value issues which are present, but less obvious, in casework, e.g. contract, manipulation, self-disclosure, recording.

(*h*) Groupwork is often exciting and rewarding, especially when the latent potential in individuals is manifest.

Models of groupwork practice

Theoretical influences

The different approaches to groupwork have been influenced by a range of theories contributing to our understanding of group behaviour, e.g. from social psychology, criminology, sociology, psychoanalytic theory, learning theory, systems theory and humanistic psychology, as well as by practitioners' own experience, creativity and responses to human need and agency function, i.e. practice-theory. Group dynamics concepts are not considered in a theoretical way in this text, and the reader is referred to Cartwright and Zander's classic (1968) and to P. Smith's more recent book (1980). For summaries of theories and research findings especially relevant to groupwork, see Hartford (1971), Douglas (1970 and 1983) and Heap (1977).

The range of models and the key variables

The term 'groupwork' subsumes a diversity of approaches to working with groups, and a number of different practice models have been developed, principally in North America, but more recently also in the UK. These models tend to overlap, and there is not as yet any generally accepted or tidy way of classifying them (Roberts and Northen, 1976).

The *practical usefulness* of any approach is basic to its acceptability, and this will depend, *inter alia*, on the level of skill needed, whether it produces desired results (effectiveness), its cost in resources and how acceptable it is likely to be to both clients and agency. Some groupwork beginners prefer the security of following a particular model or prescribed approach initially, whereas others like to start eclectically, drawing on a combination of concepts, principles and intuitive response to a particular need. Whatever the approach adopted, it is desirable to have some general idea of what you and the group are trying to achieve, the methods to be used and the underlying assumptions. There are several key variables which every group needs to address, whether it is based on a recognisable articulated model of the kind outlined below, or whether it is simply the worker's own model. These variables are:

(1) *clientele or population* – who is the group for?
(2) *setting* – what is the organisational and physical context of the group?
(3) *needs* – what need(s) is the group attempting to meet?
(4) *aims* – what is the group trying to achieve?
(5) *values* – what values and assumptions underlie this group approach?
(6) *theory* – what theoretical perspectives are being used?
(7) *practice methods* – how is the group membership determined? how is the group structured? what is the worker(s) role? how is responsibility shared between leader and members? what is the relative emphasis on the individual and on the group? what kind of programme/activities/methods are used?

The 'mainstream' models of social groupwork

These are models at the core of the social groupwork tradition (Papell and Rothman, 1980). Two of the classical and seemingly polarised earlier formulations (both usefully summarised and contrasted in Shaffer and Galinsky, 1974) are the *Michigan* (or Vinter) model and the *Schwartz* 'reciprocal' model. The former emphasises contract, programme specificity, outcome and evaluation: leadership is directive and active. The latter emphasises reciprocity, the group as a mutual aid system, and gives primacy to group process: the worker negotiates programme with the members as the group develops. Both these models have followers in contemporary groupwork (see Derricourt and Penrose, 1984 and Cooper, 1980), Schwartz probably more so than Vinter, but in recent years other models have been developed (see below).

In their 1980 article, Papell and Rothman attempt to identify the core elements in contemporary 'mainstream' groupwork, and comment that 'the conception of the group as a mutual aid system has become a universal one in all groupwork practice'. They go on to identify the following factors as core elements: negotiation of agreed goals between members and worker; spontaneously evolving group processes as the instrumental means for realising group purpose; externality (i.e. the external environment); the importance of group development; the encouragement of indigenous leadership roles and increasing group autonomy, and the great diversity of types of group and target population to be served.

These mainstream characteristics provide a useful yardstick when considering the following clusters of models which have been developed, several of them in Britain. My classification is inevitably somewhat arbitrary, but it does clarify some of the major differences in aims and in theoretical and practice emphasis.

(1) *Intake (assessment/induction) models* (Brown and Seymour, 1983, Hankinson and Stephens, 1985, Todd and Barcome, 1980). These models are relatively easily distinguished because their aims are primarily concerned with the intake process when an individual first engages with an agency, and not with specific interventions such as the provision of support, achievement of change or the amelioration of particular conditions. They are concerned in varying degrees with *group methods of individual assessment* (focus on clients) and *induction* (orientation to agency function). The groups have been used with offenders at the start of their probation or supervision orders, with prospective foster-parents, in various residential settings, and (in the USA) in walk-in crisis centres. They have potential for use in a wide range of client groups and settings, but need to be distinguished from specialised types of treatment or action groups which a person may enter at the beginning of agency contact when their particular need is already clear or obvious.

(2) *Guided group interaction models* (Stephenson and Scarpitti, 1974).

These (social control) models aim to change delinquent and ⌐
forms of anti-social behaviour into law-abiding and socially respε
sible behaviour. The theoretical basis is sociological/criminologicε
and asserts that as peer groups often provide the context for learning
deviant behaviour, attitudes and values, then by using the same process
in reverse, carefully constituted peer groups can be a vehicle for
changing behaviour from the anti-social to the law-abiding. The key
principle is to mix offenders with ex-offenders and others, the latter
exerting positive peer group pressure on the former (Cressey, 1955).
The group culture is one of openness and the methods used are highly
confrontational as well as highly supportive.

The settings are often residential or day-care establishments and
these programmes are exemplified in *positive peer culture* (Vorrath and
Brendtro, 1984) and the Phoenix House model for drug-abusers. Both
apply similar peer-confrontation principles. Some intermediate treatment groups at the 'heavy end' use this form of peer-pressure
combined with behavioural treatment methods. Apart from the philosophical and ethical issues raised, there are problems about sustaining
change when the person returns to his own social network, if the peer-
pressure there is anti- rather than pro-social.

(3) *Problem-solving, task-centred and social skills models.* This group
of models takes in quite a wide range of 'structured' approaches, all
characterised by the aims of solving specific behavioural problems,
achieving specific tasks or developing specific behavioural skills. The
behavioural emphasis is in the Michigan groupwork tradition (see, for
example, Garvin, Reid and Epstein's task-centred groupwork model,
1976) whereas the social skills model developed in Britain by Priestley,
McGuire *et al.* (1978) uses a humanistic approach based on four stages
of assessment, setting objectives, learning and evaluation. In the latter
model, learning is based on the extensive use of programmes related to
the four stages. An individual's perception and definition of his own
problem is the starting point, with a high expectation of successful
problem-solving and skill-development. It is not exclusively a group
approach as it uses a blend of individual, pairs and group methods.

Readers interested in behavioural group methods are referred to
Rose's work (1977, 1980).

(4) *Time-limited groups in the UK statutory context.* This mainstream
model in the contemporary British context was described in an article
entitled 'Towards a British Model of Groupwork' (Brown, Caddick *et
al.*, 1982). The essential elements of this approach, which is practised
quite widely in Social Services Departments, probation and some

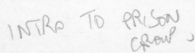
INTRO TO PRISON
GROUP

voluntary agencies (with quasi-statutory functions) were summarised as 'individual-centred aims consistent with meeting client need and carrying out agency function; an eclectic theoretical base; an overall approach which values peer sharing and mutual feedback; the creative use of a range of group techniques; co-leadership; a closed membership of from six to twelve adults (usually strangers initially, but sharing similar problems) and time-limited duration'. These groups, typical of many written up in the British social work journals, are significantly affected in their process by the organisational context and the limited time available.

(5) *Psychotherapeutic, person-focused models.* These models are characterised by their common concern with the person, his feelings, emotions and relationships. They aim to strengthen an individual's mental-health and self-concept, but the methods used and the theoretical underpinning vary considerably, from classical psycho-analytic group therapies (e.g. Slavson, 1943) to here-and-now methods (e.g. gestalt, psychodrama, TA — see below) based on humanistic growth psychologies and self-actualisation philosophies. Yalom's book on group psychotherapy (1975) offers a rich source of group therapy concepts and techniques of direct relevance to social groupwork.

Gestalt therapy (Perls, 1971) is a demanding here-and-now therapy using the 'hot seat' technique in which an individual is enabled to get in touch with immediate problematic experience and emotion, and work through the conflict or *impasse*. Other group members are involved indirectly via identification, reassurance and support. A social worker would need specialist training to take the therapist's role, as they would in the following two therapies.

Psychodrama (Blatner, 1973 and Greenberg, 1974) is a dynamic approach designed to evoke the expression of feelings involved in personal problems in a spontaneous, dramatic role-play. The main thrust of the method is to help participants relive and reformulate their problems in dramatic form in order to face their concerns directly and immediately in the living present. Experience in action, rather than words, is the touchstone. Psychodrama is a group-based model, with transferable techniques of direct use to groupworkers (see Chapter 4, which also describes *sociodrama*).

Transactional Analysis (Pitman, 1984) is an example of a specific technique developed with individuals, but now often practised in groups. The basis concept of the parent-adult-child ego-structure is quickly grasped and, like psychodrama, it is a technique which can be drawn on and practised at whatever level the practitioner has reached. The potential of TA has not yet been fully developed as a group technique, the group often being little more than an arena for individual 'work'.

(6) *Self-help, mutual support models* (Brimelow and Wilson, 1982; Lindenfield and Adams, 1984; Silverman, 1980). This type of group is largely self-governing and provides its members with a source of mutual help and support. Alcoholics Anonymous is an example of a long-established fully autonomous self-help group. There has been a rapid growth of self-help groups in recent years covering almost every kind of human need, including: socially oppressed minorities, e.g. black women's groups; shared health problems, e.g. mastectomy groups, agoraphobic groups; 'linked-fate' groups (Whitaker, 1985), e.g. carers' groups, parents of handicapped children; consumers of social services groups, e.g. NAYPIC, foster-parents' groups – the list is endless.

There are also many 'in-between' or quasi self-help groups where the social worker has some role-relationship with the group, at least for a while. This role may involve her in *negotiating* with agencies or for resources on behalf of the group, *mediating* between members, *facilitating* the development of group cohesion, *clarification* of roles, *conflict-resolution*, acting as *consultant*, and many other roles. Brimelow and Wilson's articles provide a useful guide to the often sensitive role and function of the professional social worker in relation to the self-help group.

(7) *Social goals models* (Button, 1974, D. N. Thomas, 1978, Mullender and Ward, 1985). There are several models, mostly developed in the youth and community work context, which cluster in this category. They are all characterised by goals external to the group and concerned with some form of social development and social change. The models can be differentiated according to the emphasis on *process* (the effect group participation itself has on the members, e.g. increased self-confidence) or *product* (practical gains which the group achieves, e.g. some new neighbourhood resource), and according to the degree of *politicisation* and *structural change* associated with both aims and methods. Button's model is an example of *developmental groupwork*, targeted on 'ordinary' children and adolescents in their own community. Community action groups, more akin to community work, are neighbourhood groups which identify and work to achieve defined environmental changes, e.g. tenants' associations pressing for children's play facilities.

Mullender and Ward have recently conceptualised a *self-directed* model of groupwork. It is described as 'essentially a hybrid' containing elements of problem-centred, social education and self-help groups, but with the crucial difference that it is primarily concerned with changes external to the group. Members are drawn from categories for whom social agencies have direct and often legal responsibility, but the emphasis is on issue-based campaigning. The model is self-directed, in that once the group has formed, the workers accept a commitment to achieve external change on issues put forward by group members. How this is combined with social control functions has not yet been fully clarified.

Human relations training groups (Smith, 1980)

These groups are concerned with here-and-now 'sensitivity training' for practitioners from various professions whose work involves them in group leadership and membership. They are *not* a social groupwork model to be used in social work agencies when working with clients, but are included here because of their value in developing the groupworker's own personal awareness of the less obvious, sometimes unconscious processes which affect all groups and their capacity to carry out their tasks. The value of sensitivity groups as a training experience is discussed in Chapter 5.

Models used for this purpose include Tavistock, T-groups and en-counter models, and excellent summaries of these approaches can be found in Shaffer and Galinsky (1974).

Groupwork in residential and day-care settings

Many of the groupwork models outlined above and the basic groupwork skills and processes described in the rest of this book, can be adapted to work with groups in residential and day-care settings (see for example Lennox, 1982). There are, however, some fundamental differences deriving from the group-living context, which are well described in some residential work texts (Clough, 1982), but not usually from a 'working with groups' perspective. One exception is a useful paper by Payne (1978) in which he suggests that groupwork knowledge and skills are needed in many areas of residential practice, and he identifies some of these as: managing the natural resources of group living; coping with daily tensions; integration of new arrivals; preparation for leaving; and facilitation of personal growth, problem-solving and social functioning. In a brief article, Mounsey (1983) applies Yalom's eleven curative group factors (1975, Chapter 1) to the whole living environment of a mental health day-centre.

Residential and day-care settings have a rich mosaic (or chaotic jumble?!) of many different kinds of groups and groupings including:

(1) informal friendship/affinity groups
(2) living together groupings, e.g. for eating, sleeping, leisure
(3) group living issues groups for staff and residents, e.g. house, unit and community meetings
(4) structured closed groups for specific purposes, e.g. art therapy, social skills, behaviour modification
(5) staff groups and groupings, formal and informal
(6) groups for particular events either inside, e.g. plays, assemblies, parties, or outside, e.g. outings, trips
(7) groups which embrace both insiders and outsiders, e.g. family groups, case conferences, groups which include people from the local community.

Residents and staff will have simultaneous (and sometimes frequently changing) membership of several of these groups and groupings at any given time, so that when any group is together its membership brings to it a range of other shared experience, knowledge, attitudes, feelings, allegiances and expectations which will profoundly affect group process and group task. This makes issues such as consistency, continuity, boundary, task, role and confidentiality extremely important, as is an understanding of large groups and inter-group processes (see McCaughan, 1977).

With no comprehensive conceptualisation of this mosaic as yet available to guide them, residential and day-care staff are left with the task of working out for themselves how they can adapt and make most effective use of the skills and concepts of social groupwork to suit their particular needs and work contexts. There are a few places in this book where these contexts are explicitly referred to or illustrated, but elsewhere the basic concepts about, for example, group size and composition, contract, stages of group development, leadership, co-working, problematic roles and stuck groups are there for the reader to make use of as appropriate in her own setting.

Summary on models

A wide range of approaches is included loosely under the term 'groupwork' and it is possible to cluster models and methods in various ways. The practice guidelines in the following chapters are not based on one particular model. The emphasis will be on basic skills and processes which apply to most groups and can be adapted by practitioners to suit different settings, styles and needs.

Values and ethics

A survey of the groupwork literature reveals very little written explicitly about values and ethics (but see Bernstein, 1972). For a recent discussion of BASW's Code of Ethics see Watson (1985). Some issues, including confidentiality, self-determination, leader-style and group pressure, have a uniquely group dimension. Every groupworker will have a personal value-stance which will influence groups that she works with. As Bernstein states, there is no such thing as value-neutrality in groupwork, or indeed in social work. Every action and communication, whether verbal or non-verbal, says something about the worker's values. (Those of the author will be evident in this book.) The first question might be 'How clear is the groupworker about her own values, and how explicitly does she, and should she, share them with those she works with?' There are many important value and ethical issues, some of which are discussed below.

Art or science?

In his philosophical allegory *Zen and the Art of Motor-Cycle Maintenance*, Pirsig (1976) distinguished two stereotypes of the motor-cycle enthusiast. One is the person who is a first-rate mechanic and excels in the technical aspects of motor cycles and their maintenance. He understands how they work and can repair them when they go wrong. As he rides along he is conscious of how well the engine is functioning. His stance is 'classical'. The second type of motor-cyclist gets his satisfaction and delight from the experience of riding the machine at speed along country roads on a beautiful day. He feels the air and senses the sounds and smells. If there is a mechanical fault, he takes it to the nearest garage. His stance is 'romantic'.

  The social-science equivalents of these two positions are logical positivist and existentialist respectively. In groupwork terms the former is concerned with specific goals, detailed programme, clear roles, defined structure and evaluation of outcome. The latter views the process itself as being of paramount importance, the experience providing its own validation. Each social worker will be at some point on this science–art continuum. Pirsig's resolution of the apparent conflict is integration at a higher level he calls 'quality'. Perhaps high-quality groupwork involves taking an interest in both what people experience *and* what they achieve.

The use of power and self-determination

We have already seen how different models and approaches to group-work reflect different ideological and political positions. In one dimension 'person-changing' and 'system-changing' practitioners are at opposite poles, but they are both exercising their power to try to influence others, individually or collectively, in directions they desire. How prepared is either of them to be changed herself by the power of the group and its members?

One social worker, working with a group of boys from a delinquent sub-culture, was surprised to find over a period of time that instead of the boys' attitudes changing, her own were being changed. To her dismay, she was gradually becoming converted to the logic of their delinquent life-style. She complained that no one had warned her about that on her training course! By contrast, in the group-therapy scene in *One Flew Over the Cuckoo's Nest* (Kesey, 1973), the nursing sister ruthlessly exercises her institutionally based power to reduce individual patients' power and ensure conformity on the ward. A more group-oriented leader might have 'allowed' the group to be a context for each man to discover the source and nature of his own and the group's power. This could have led to pressure for changes in the hospital regime and, undoubtedly, the particular hospital depicted so graphically by Ken Kesey would rapidly have sacked the sister or terminated the group in such circumstances!

What kind of morality?

Each social worker has some kind of personal moral code or ethic, be it Christian, humanist, Marxist, or a pragmatic mixture of these and other ideologies. Some approaches to groupwork are explicitly linked to a particular moral position. An example of this is reality therapy, an approach developed by William Glasser (1965) and used in schools and residential work. The aim is to inculcate defined moral standards, and the practitioner is expected to have, and to proclaim in the group, a definite commitment based on these principles.

Many moral perspectives converge in the belief that there is latent potential in each individual, and that a group can be a catalyst for developing personal resources and abilities. An example of this occurred in a long-sentence prison group. Two of the members were serving life sentences for the attempted murder of their wives, and both faced the agonising problem of maintaining relationships with their children whilst in prison. One was a quite well-educated man, and the other was regarded as illiterate and stupid by prisoners and staff alike. In one session when the first man was rationalising about not allowing his children to visit on the grounds of protecting them from pain, the other man, drawing on his own personal experiences and with great sensitivity, helped the first to see that in fact it was himself and his own painful feelings that he was protecting. As a consequence of this very moving interchange, contact with the first man's children was gradually renewed.

What is confidential in a group?

There are two ways in which confidentiality can be a special problem in groups. The first, particularly in a statutory agency, concerns what the social worker does with the information about individuals which emerges in a group. Does she pass it on to other colleagues who may have referred a client, does she record it in the personal file or does she maintain complete secrecy? The second concerns what any one group member does with information about any of the others. Each member has a right to know the answers to these questions, because they will affect his freedom to trust, take risks and divulge personal information about himself or others.

Considering that only the leader is bound by a professional ethic, it is surprising how often confidentiality *is* respected in groups. This may be because although group members' confidentiality ethic is discretionary rather than absolute, it is often acceptable in the relevant culture. One safeguard is to have open discussions about it at the group contract-making stage, and to establish a working agreement which is accepted by all. When a group session and activities are to be recorded in sound or video, group members' agreement would normally be sought *and* a clear undertaking given of the purpose of such a recording and the limitations on its use. If an agency requires the leader to pass on certain types of information either verbally or in agency records, then members should know this, and can then act accordingly. Another advantage of making this clear in the contract is that when something very personal or controversial is divulged, members can if necessary be reminded of the agreement. In groupwork, the gains of collective responsibility and mutual helping carry with them the risks of indiscretion and abuse.

Is there a hidden agenda?

Groupwork varies in the extent to which there is an open culture. The style adopted by the leader will often be a role-model for others. The manipulative leader with her hidden agenda cannot expect a group full of open, trusting members! There are many advantages in openness and the onus is on the worker to find very good reasons for any secrecy. There may be occasions when damaged or disturbed people need protection from openness, but the worker needs to consider very carefully whether it is not herself or her agency she is really trying to protect with her hidden agenda (which is not to say that social workers do not have very real needs for protection too). The contract approach discussed in the next chapter reflects the 'open' ethic.

Should group membership always be voluntary?

This is a difficult question facing social workers in statutory agencies. Many of the activities, contacts and decisions in statutory social work involve varying degrees of coercive behaviour by social workers. Is mandatory group membership of a different order of coercion? A young person in a community home has to do many things required by the staff and the regime, and it could be said that participation in formal groups is no different from playing football, attending craft workshops, maths classes or individual counselling sessions. In a country with compulsory education up to the age of sixteen, this would at least be consistent. But what of the thirty-year-old woman on probation? Should she have more choice about whether she joins a social skills group than whether she meets her probation officer individually? Should she know, when she agrees to be placed on probation, that this is a commitment to participate in some type of activity, but with choice among those available? There are no easy answers to these questions, not least because in many situations the distinction between voluntary and compulsory is blurred. An old lady in an elderly persons' home wants to choose not to take part in group discussions about preparation for death; a fifteen-year-old wants to opt out of a group discussion on personal relationships at an IT camp; a parent of a child on a supervision order would prefer not to join a parent-effectiveness group: each might suspect that although a choice is offered, refusal to comply could have adverse consequences and repercussions.

One guiding principle that *can* be applied generally is maximum clarity and openness about whether there *is* a real choice about (a) joining or (b) opting out. When people are compelled to join a group this has consequences in the group which are sometimes (but not necessarily always) negative.

Can groups be damaging to individuals?

It is axiomatic that any activity or experience which has potential for beneficial change also has potential for unhelpful or even damaging change. One issue is whether individuals at risk can be identified and protected by exclusion or safeguards. Another is the quality of leadership and acceptability of the method. Most of the research which has been done on the subject (Lieberman, Yalom and Miles, 1973; Galinsky and Schopler, 1977) has been done on T-groups and encounter groups, and often with student populations. This makes generalisation about other types of groups and populations problematic.

The study reported by Lieberman *et al.* was on the effects of encounter groups on Stanford students. About 8 per cent of the sample were rated as 'casualties' as a direct result of group participation. The 'mechanisms of injury' included attacks by leader or group; rejection by leader or group; failure to attain unrealistic goals; coercive expectations; and input overload or 'value shuffle'. This research has been criticised on methodological and other grounds but some of the findings may at least serve as pointers to groupworkers in other contexts.

The leader has a responsibility not to attack or reject individuals, but gentle confrontation and almost any intervention can be experienced subjectively by an individual as attack or rejection if he is feeling under pressure and low in self-esteem. The setting of realistic and achievable goals is desirable, as is sensitivity about challenges to other people's value systems. Care in group composition is another safeguard, but with natural groups and groups in residential settings, the worker often has no choice. The positive leadership qualities which minimise the likelihood of damage to individuals are outlined in Chapter 3.

There are no clear answers to most of the value and ethical issues discussed here. Each practitioner faces these issues within the general framework of personal and social work ethics.

2. Planning a Group: Preparation and Contract

This chapter is about what takes place before the first meeting of a group. The importance of this stage in groupwork cannot be over-estimated. Research evidence (Douglas, 1970) and practice experience both testify that effectiveness or 'success' (however defined) are determined as much by what happens *before* the group comes into existence, as by what happens during the group's life. The preparation stages may lack the demands, enjoyment and involvement of actual group meetings and activities, but they require just as much creative energy, clear thinking and skill in communication. Some groups are stillborn or die later because social workers underestimate the time and care which good preparation requires.

The idea of forming a group, or working with an existing one, usually comes from one or more individuals who may be potential group members, individual social workers, the team or senior agency staff. Whoever first thought of the group is likely to have a special investment in it which will influence the subsequent course of events, during preparation and as the group develops. Another factor will be the reactions of others to the perceived motives of the initiators. Thus preparation for a group is not only a straightforward rational procedure, but a process which is affected by people's feelings and reactions to each other as well as to the proposal itself.

Planning and preparation for a group includes three stages, which often overlap. Firstly, the groupworker must be satisfied that a need or problem exists and is shared by a number of people for whom some common aim can be identified. She must also be satisfied that a group is more likely than other available methods to meet the need and achieve the aim. She should be able to commit the outline scheme to paper.

Secondly, the organisational and environmental context of the group must be assessed to see whether there is sufficient support to make the group worth attempting. This 'sounding out' or feasibility study includes preliminary negotiations with persons and groups in the agency (and elsewhere if necessary) who are in influential positions and whose support is needed. These may include management staff who control resources needed for the group, and colleagues whose clients are potential group members.

Thirdly, the actual process of creating the group will be undertaken, if the indications from the previous stages are positive. This stage involves obtaining resources, recruiting a membership and making initial decisions about time, place and duration. It also includes making arrangements for consultation, and negotiating a preliminary contract or working agreement with members.

Perspectives on aims and expectations

The range of possible aims for different groups was outlined in the previous chapter. In a statutory agency there are likely to be differing aims for the same group. Aplin (1977) has distinguished the *agency perspective*, the *practice perspective* and the *client perspective*. These three perspectives will often differ and a viable group requires not that they be identical, but that there are sufficient common elements. It also requires a reasonable convergence of perspective *within* each category, i.e. as between potential members and as between group leaders and relevant colleagues. The following example illustrates the possible variation in perspectives, even when there is apparently common agreement on needs and goals.

> *Example*: A Social Services Department District Office decides to form a group for lone parents, with an associated playgroup for their children. The aim is stated in general terms as a support group for lone parents to help them manage more easily. Whilst nearly everyone subscribes to this rather vague aim, perceptions of what it really means vary considerably.

Firstly, we may consider the *agency perspective*. The agency has faced some criticism about the number of children from one-parent families being taken into care. Funds for preventive work are available, and this type of group is seen as an effective form of prevention. It would also be an opportunity to keep a closer watch on several families under suspicion for child-abuse, and to make sure that the children get a proper midday meal. The parents could be taught practical things concerned with home management, social skills and caring for the children. The Area Director is keen to have parents' groups in each of her districts, as they are increasing elsewhere in the county and currently favoured by the Department. The team leader is a group-work enthusiast and sees the group as a way of putting her team on the map as a progressive multi-method unit.

The social workers illustrate the *practice perspective*. They will be directly involved with establishing and running the group, and have various motives for supporting it, including a conviction that group-work is more effective than casework for helping these families; a wish to increase their own groupwork experience and skills; a belief that having a thriving group will enhance the status of their team; and a hope that they can be more influential with their clients and improve the standards of child-care, emotionally and physically. It will also make a welcome change from the round of home visits, and hopefully establish better relationships with the families.

The *client perspective* is similarly varied. Some of the parents, especially those regularly visited by a social worker, see this group as a new means of checking up on their treatment of their children. They feel under some pressure to join, as the social workers have powers to take their children into care. On the other hand, it would be nice to have the children looked after by someone else one morning a week, and to have the opportunity to sit around and talk with other parents. There is the added attraction of a cheap lunch and free coffee. Some are hoping to make new friends. One hopes that if she attends regularly she may be able to get her eldest child back from the foster parents. Some hope that going to the group will be a support and help them in trying to cope with their children and family responsibilities.

When there is a general aim, as in this example, expectations are more likely to be divergent. One way of attempting to get more con-sensus about expectations is to be more specific about aims. This will not remove the different perspectives illustrated above, but it can provide a baseline for identifying variations at the contract-making stage when time spent 'clearing expectations' often pays dividends later. This can be repeated at intervals during the life of the group, but becomes less necessary when the members themselves are actively involved in planning and leadership. In some 'reciprocal' approaches, the groupworker is deliberately non-specific about aims at the pre-group stages, leaving scope for the group itself to decide on goals at its first meeting.

The group and its environment

As Whitaker (1976) has stated, 'A group is more likely to be successful if it is conducted in an organisation or institutional context in which other personnel, not directly involved with the group, nevertheless accept and support its aims and general procedures, and value its potential contribution to the shared goals of the institution or organisation.' This means that at a very early stage the social worker has to assess the environmental context of any group she is considering establishing. If there is a positive tradition and wide acceptance of groupwork in the organisation, all is well, and routine procedures are followed. If, on the other hand, groupwork is either new or has to contend with an unhappy past history of organisational indifference or even hostility, then preparation of the environment is essential, and may take a long time and much hard work.

Three organisational settings will now be considered: the non social work oriented institution, the residential social work establishment and the fieldwork setting. Day-care settings combine features of both residential and fieldwork, and will not be considered separately.

The non social work oriented institution

Anyone who has attempted groupwork in a prison, hospital or school setting, will be aware of the power of the institutional forces, and how dependent the groupworker is on the co-operation of non social work staff. Two examples illustrate this.

> *Example*:   The first meeting of a prison group is held in a room on the education wing. The group has been carefully planned and has the approval of the Governor and Chief Officer. The two leaders are sitting waiting for the prison officers to bring the group members from their wing in another part of the prison. No one comes. Eventually one of the leaders, who is a prison welfare officer, sets off angrily to the wing, only to be told on arrival that the prison officers 'didn't know' about the group meeting. At last, the group meeting starts but it gets interrupted by prison officers opening the door from time to time, and staring through the window. When the group ends, the leaders and the members have to run the gauntlet of officers in the passage and a senior officer says in a voice all can hear, 'You're wasting your bloody time with these buggers, they'll never change.' This group survived the test and was allowed to function relatively smoothly thereafter. More significantly, it paved the way for other groups to follow. Some recent (unpublished) experience in prisons where prison officers are directly involved in leading social skills groups for men approaching discharge, has indicated the potential strength of institutional support and involvement.

Example: A therapy group is suggested in a state psychiatric hospital in the USA with no recent tradition of a group approach. A social worker and a psychologist, both quite recently appointed to the hospital staff, endeavour to start a group-therapy programme. This is not approved of by medical staff committed to the individual treatment model, and groups are frequently interrupted when particular patients are 'needed' for dance therapy, injections and other diversionary treatments.

These illustrations, perhaps rather daunting but not particularly unusual, indicate the need to create 'space' for a group in such an institution by preparing the ground carefully and attempting to gain enough support at least to protect the outer boundary of the group from external 'sabotage'. Many people have fantasies and fears about groups and their power, and preparation time spent working through some of these feelings, as well as discussing all the practical and organisational problems, usually pays dividends.

The other extreme to institutional opposition is institutional pro-group policies where the norm is to have groups on all wards, wings or houses. Where this forms part of a coherent, well thought-out therapeutic milieu, as in the prototype of the Henderson hospital (M. Jones, 1953), and Grendon Underwood prison, the environmental support structure is invaluable. Where it is a policy imposed on a largely unwilling staff and residents, it becomes counter-productive and liable to discredit the contribution of groupwork.

The residential social work establishment (see also p.20)

In residential group-living settings, which are part of social work provision (e.g. community homes, probation hostels) and which are staffed and run by residential social workers, any groups which are formed need to be part of an integrated programme.

Example: In the USA some residential establishments for young offenders have adopted the 'positive peer culture' approach (Vorrath and Brendtro, 1984) which focuses on a set group meeting for one and a half hours each evening, with the rest of the day spent on education, PE, work and leisure activities. The strength of the approach (which can be criticised on other grounds) is that the formal group session is consciously and consistently related to the rest of the entire programme, and vice versa. All the staff (whether teacher, cook, groupworker, PE instructor or director) have a commitment to an integrated approach, so the group meetings which are primarily based on peer influence have all the advantages of institutional support and consistency.

The fieldwork setting

Here the influence of the agency environment on a groupwork proposal is perhaps less obvious than in an institutional setting, but it can be equally powerful. This is illustrated by the experience of one CQSW course which encourages students to seek opportunities to work with groups during a six-month fieldwork placement. A pattern has emerged indicating that whether or not a student gets some groupwork experience on placement is at least as dependent on the prevailing attitudes in the agency and team as it is on the needs and motivation of the clients, or the commitment and skills of the students.

The agency environment in general

Indicators of a supportive agency environment for groupwork include the availability of money and other resources; availability of supervision and consultation; recognition of groupwork in workload calculations; collaboration from colleagues in 'sharing' clients, co-leading groups and providing emotional support; and an agency climate which values social workers using creative means to achieve statutory ends (McCaughan, 1985; Laming and Sturton, 1978). These 'ideal' conditions often take years to establish, but if the climate is favourable much can be achieved.

It is not possible to lay down specific procedures or strategies to be followed when groupwork is not widely accepted in an agency or institution, because each context is different, but most approaches include the following:

(a) seeking the support of colleagues in the team,
(b) consulting with middle-managers, enabling them to understand more about your project, express their views and feel involved,
(c) producing written information about the proposed group, its aims and requirements, and how these (e.g. resources, accommodation, shared clients, community involvement) may affect others in the agency,
(d) being sensitive to the feelings of others. Groups are still perceived by many people as rather threatening and mysterious, especially in teams based on traditional casework approaches. It is important that colleagues who prefer other approaches are not made to feel excluded or inferior in status. Open opposition is much easier to respond to than a mixture of verbal support ('I think your group is a good idea') and contradictory actions ('I never seem to have anyone suitable for your group on my caseload').

Note that these approaches assume a consensus model. More radical approaches to change are discussed by Resnick and Patti (1980).

The social environment

In addition to the agency environment, groups are influenced by the social environment of the participants. All potential leaders and members of a social work group are also members of other groups and alliances in their own social settings. Examples of these are families, friendship groups, schoolmates, work groups and gangs. These primary groups constitute part of the social environment systems which influence decisions about group membership and participation.

> *Example*:   An activity/social education group for ten- to twelve-year-old children with behaviour difficulties. As this group is to be held during school hours, the groupworkers are dependent on the co-operation of both teachers and parents. The group has much more chance of getting started and becoming useful for each child if it is at least tolerated, if not actively supported by the primary environments of home and school. If there is opposition, the child is in constant role conflict about joining the group and attending sessions.

> *Example*:   An activity group for young offenders. For the first meeting the probation officer has recruited four members, three who know each other and a fourth, Jim, who is a member of another gang. Half-way through the first session the other members of that gang arrive quite unexpectedly, requesting that Jim leave the group and go with them, which he does meekly before the leader or members can do anything about it.

> *Example*: Two social workers, male and female colleagues, co-lead a therapeutic group from 6.30 to 8.00 on Monday evenings. The man is single and his girl-friend, being a nurse, understands about evening work (though she wishes he would take time off in lieu!). He gets her support and feels it within him when planning and leading the group. His female colleague is married with two children and feels constantly under pressure because her children expect her home in the evening, and so does her husband (not a social worker) who resents the intimacy of the 'professional marriage' which she and her colleague need for effective co-leadership of the group. The husband has feelings of exclusion from this social work activity which he cannot really understand and which sometimes seems more a way of life than a job to be done.

The physical environment

Groups are also affected by the physical environment in which meetings and activities take place. Firstly, there are the connotations a particular room has for each person, e.g. health clinic, pub, probation office, youth club, deaf institute, community centre. Secondly, there is the direct impact of the physical layout and its suitability for a particular purpose. Studies in proxemics (the study of personal and social space) have shown that human communication is much influenced by physical spacing and distance (Hall, 1969). Thirdly, familiar territory has a supportive and reassuring function for a group and changes of territory in mid-group can have an unsettling effect.

Resources and finance

Because groups always involve a number of people and often use activities, they require resources of various kinds. The availability or otherwise of resources says something about the priority groupwork is given by an agency. If groupwork is seen as an integral method of social work intervention, the resources should be there, whereas if it is viewed as an optional extra then the material response is likely to be cheese-paring and reluctant. A basic groupwork skill is that of obtaining the necessary resources. This is not easy, and the agency may directly or indirectly expect the social workers to furnish evidence that the group will be effective and the money well spent. Perhaps because groupwork is more visible than casework, official expectations of pay-off and cost-effectiveness tend to be higher, placing additional pressure on the social workers concerned. There are several necessary resources which are considered below.

Time

Groupwork involves considerable expenditure of social worker time, and the amount is often underestimated. It appears more economical to see eight people all together than each separately, but the arithmetic is more complicated than that! Firstly, there is the time needed for planning the group, and all the various negotiations that are necessary. Secondly, there is the time involved directly in the sessions themselves. This might be one or two hours each week, plus, in some groups, block periods of weekends or several weekdays for particular activities such as camps, outings, social skills training or therapeutic workshops. Thirdly, time is needed between sessions for planning, reviewing, recording, obtaining resources, and meeting with a consultant and/or co-leader. Fourthly, time may also be needed between sessions for meeting with members individually, visiting absentees and other significant persons in their family and social networks.

The total time needed for a group varies widely according to type, but for each group an estimate can be made, allowing for the various extra-group commitments. This expenditure of time should be allowed for in exactly the same way as any other work commitments. If groupwork involves evening or weekend work, then time should be allowed in lieu. This may seem obvious, but often does not happen.

Staff

A groupwork programme, whether in a residential, day-care or community setting, requires staff who are motivated to commit time and skill and to take on leadership roles. Many groups need two leaders and sometimes additional ancillary or volunteer help with transport, creches, camping and various specialist activities. It also requires staff who are willing and able to offer consultation and supervision to social workers undertaking groupwork.

Skill

Groupwork is a skilled activity and any agency which offers groupwork to clients needs to invest resources in groupwork skill development for staff. This may involve mounting in-service training programmes and funding staff to take relevant post-qualifying courses outside the agency. It may also mean paying external consultants, or appointing internal consultant staff to develop groupwork in the agency.

Accommodation

The impact of the physical environment on a group and its well-being has already been referred to. Unfortunately, for many practitioners, the question 'What are the best surroundings for this group?' is rather academic because they are struggling to find any accommodation at all. There are very few agencies that provides group rooms, so existing rooms have to be adapted from their primary purpose, or accommodation has to be sought in the community, and begged, borrowed or hired.

Accommodation considerations include the following.

(a) Physical requirements. How much space is needed? How many rooms? Can boisterous, messy, noisy activities be done? Is a carpet needed? Is there a kitchen or at least coffee-making facilities? Are toilets available? Is outside space needed?
(b) Geographical location. Is the place reasonably accessible to the members, and near to public transport routes?
(c) Venue. Is agency or neutral territory preferred?

(*d*) Cost. Is there a budget allowance for renting accommodation?

(*e*) Boundary protection. Whether agency or non-agency property, the accommodation is likely to be shared with other groups and used for other purposes. It is important to ensure that the group's time boundary is protected at both ends, and the physical boundary protected during sessions. This may be difficult when a group is located in a large residential establishment or in part of a large busy agency building, but interruption, whether innocent or 'sabotage', can be very disrupting.

(*f*) Using what you have. E.g. a social worker with an adolescent group had no alternative but to meet in a room that was used as a juvenile court. This was exploited by a very successful sociodrama session re-enacting a court scene.

Facilities and equipment

Groups vary in their requirements for equipment, from chairs or cushions for a discussion group, to workshops and sports equipment for some activity groups, to video equipment for social skills training groups. Groupworkers often have to work hard obtaining funds even for coffee and orange squash, never mind the more expensive items. Negotiating and advocacy skills are needed, short-term for obtaining the facilities for any one group, and long-term for influencing agency policy on groupwork equipment and funds. In some groups, members themselves can contribute or obtain resources, and this can be a way of sharing responsibility for the group.

Transport

Groups may need transport for two purposes. One is to get people to the group sessions, the other is for group activities, e.g. outdoor pursuits. The former is not just a question of resources, it also involves assessment of need and the desirability or otherwise of fostering dependency. Transport at the door can be an essential help to a mother with young children, whereas in other circumstances it can diminish personal responsibility and choice about whether or not to attend a group meeting.

Group composition, size, time and selection

When the need for a group has been identified, objectives clarified, and resources obtained, the next concerns are its composition, size and the selection of members and leaders. Each of these will be considered in turn, drawing on theoretical guidelines where these are available, as well as practice experience. There are aspects of group composition on which theorists diverge, but there are also some guidelines which have general support (Hartford, 1971; Yalom, 1975). The evidence on group size is more clear-cut because this is a single variable about which fairly confident predictions can be made. By contrast, most theorists say little or nothing about selection criteria for group leaders.

Group composition

The key decisions in group composition are concerned with homogeneity and heterogeneity, balance and compatibility. Redl's law of 'optimum distance' states that groups should be 'homogeneous enough to ensure stability, and heterogeneous enough to ensure vitality' (1951). Homogeneity is needed to develop group cohesion, and heterogeneity is necessary to produce the forces for change in a group. The emphasis will depend on whether the aim of the group is primarily change, or support.

The need for balance requires that on any continuum of attributes, no individual is too far removed from at least one other, e.g. it is not generally a good idea to have one person who is twenty years older (or younger) than anyone else, or who is the only one of his or her sex, or who is the only person from a particular race, social class or culture. Every new group member has a need for compatibility (complementary needs and mutual liking) with at least one other member.

A useful way of thinking about group composition is outlined by Bertcher and Maple (1977) in their manual *Creating Groups*. Drawing on research, they developed an approach based on homogeneity of *descriptive attributes* and heterogeneity of *behavioural attributes*.

Descriptive attributes are factual descriptions of an individual, e.g. woman, black, middle-aged, physically disabled, each of which carries associated role-positions, status and stereotypes, which will have a profound influence on group interaction and that individual's role in the group. Hare (1962) refers to research indicating that people with higher social status in the community who attend a group tend to participate more and take more aggressive roles (and conversely). Key descriptive attributes include the following:

(a) *Age.* Most writers favour a limited age-range, especially for children's and adolescents' groups, bringing together people at a similar developmental stage. Variations on this are family groups where membership of the family system is the criterion, and problem-focused groups where another descriptive attribute is more significant than age (see (d) below).

(b) *Gender*.   Early studies of groups with mixed and same-sex composition drew some tentative conclusions about the ways in which sex composition can affect group process and outcome. They suggested, for instance, that there are advantages in single-sex groups for children and younger adolescents (Hartford, 1971) and that mixed-sex groups for adults tend to be more concerned about interpersonal relations and hence conform more than members of same-sex groups which concentrate on task (Shaw, 1976). It is only more recently, however, that the significance of sexism and sex-stereotyping for group behaviour in mixed groups and same-sex groups has become a subject for serious study, and the reader is referred to a special issue of the journal *Social Work with Groups* on gender issues in social groupwork practice (Reed and Garvin, 1983).

(c) *Race, class and culture*.   After surveying the literature and practice experience, Hartford (1971) concludes '... when the group composition anticipated is racially, ethnically or socio-economically mixed, it is well to have a clear purpose, preferably focused on task'. She goes on to suggest that groups composed on a basis of racial and/or social class differences are likely to involve more effort in the group-creation stage, and also to require more directive leadership by the worker in the early stages of group development. As with gender and sexism, it is only recently that serious attention has been given to relating racial composition in groupwork to the wider context of racism, stereotyping and white power. Davis (1980 and 1984), a black groupworker writer in the North American context, opens up these issues, drawing attention for example to the significance of the numerical ratio of black and white members in mixed groups. He hypothesises the concept of the 'psychological majority' to explain the shifts which occur in groups when the black–white ratio exceeds the outside norm, even if blacks still comprise no more than half the group membership numerically. He also stresses the importance of white leaders of racially mixed groups having a basic understanding of the impact that black history, racism and environmental factors will have on group dynamics and process. Smith (1985) has also drawn together some of the British and US research on this subject.

(d) *Type of problem/life situation*.   Some in this category are fairly clearly descriptive attributes, e.g. prisoner, lone father, parent of a handicapped child, non-attender at school, foster parent. Others are more subjective and behaviourally labelled, e.g. depressive, delinquent, social isolate.

Behavioural attributes refer to the ways in which individuals actually behave (past and present), their personality, attitudes and life-styles. Behaviours are, of course, much influenced by context and by role-expectations associated with descriptive attributes, but for a given 'set', individuals do vary behaviourally on a range of continua, e.g. task orientation – relationship orientation (Bales, 1950), talkative–quiet, submissive–dominant, leader–follower, initiator–reactor, introvert–extrovert, fighter–appeaser, spontaneous–controlled. Any group concerned with change needs variety in the range of behaviours, skills and experiences which the members (and the workers) bring, combined with sufficient commonality of basic descriptive attributes.

Bertcher and Maple (1977) state that *effective* groups are those in which members are interactive (talk to each other freely); compatible (show that they like one another); and responsive (interested and active in helping and being helped). *Barriers* to effective groups include too much compatibility; too much or too little stress; too few role-models; and negative sub-groups.

The following examples were drawn from a voluntary agency specialising in groupwork with lone parents.

Example: A short-life 'closed' discussion group was composed of separated and divorced mothers bringing up children on their own, and not employed. Both leaders were also female. The homogeneity of descriptive attributes (female, separated or divorced, parent, non-employed) was reinforced by behavioural homogeneity, in that all the women were rather depressed. There was an atmosphere of 'sameness' reinforced by having two female leaders. There was a lack of initiators and extroverts, and no obvious work-leaders or role-models. This group struggled to develop at all, due to too much similarity, and too little stimulation to change.

Example: A short-life 'closed' discussion group was composed of widowed, separated and divorced fathers, bringing up children on their own, some employed and some unemployed. There was a mixed social class background, and male/female co-leaders. This group was less descriptively homogeneous than the previous one, but the combination of basic descriptive similarity, i.e. fathers bringing up children alone, plus variations in personality and life-style, two or three convincing and optimistic role-models, and a female co-leader, all seemed to promote a sounder basis of group composition and a more effective group (as rated by consumer feedback) than in the previous example.

These two groups were not evaluated in any systematic way but the contrasting outcomes are consistent with the Bertcher and Maple guidelines. An invaluable asset, which can sometimes be planned, is having one or two members in a group who take responsibility at an early stage, setting an example to others and enhancing group motivation and commitment.

Finally, there is the important distinction between groups composed of strangers, and groups containing some or all members who already know each other and the leader. In natural groups, and groups in residential and day-care settings, people are already in some relationship with one another, and that is a given circumstance to be worked with. In field settings, there is the possibility of choice.

Having some members who are previously acquainted can be beneficial if those relationships are basically positive and open, lending the group stability and a growth point. Conversely, antagonistic or cliquey acquaintances can disrupt or unbalance a new group.

Members with previous or continuing individual relationships with the leader or leaders can face difficulties, particularly when the leader is in some authority or assessment role, and issues of confidentiality arise. A group with only one member in that position is not recommended as it puts undue pressure on that individual. Two or more are in a stronger position. A group in which either none or all have known the leader previously is often not practicable with generic caseloads.

Group size

The information on group size available from small group research (Hartford, 1971) is firm enough to be useful for practitioners. If we assume the minimum size of a small group to be three members and the maximum about twelve the following factors are associated with increasing size in this range:

(*a*) The number of one-to-one relationships increases rapidly, e.g. three pairs in a three-person group, fifteen in a six-person group, thirty-six in a nine-person group.

(*b*) Sub-groupings are more likely (especially from eight members upwards).

(*c*) 'Physical freedom is restricted, while psychological freedom is increased' (Slater, 1958). In larger groups there is less space and time for each person, but more freedom to rest or be inconspicuous, and more opportunity to identify with other role-models. (In very small groups of three or four, individuals may be over-exposed and under-stimulated.)

(*d*) Problem-solving takes longer, but may produce better solutions.

(e) More specific roles tend to emerge, and be highlighted.

(f) The very active and talkative members become more so, and conversely, the reticent become less likely to participate (see Chapter 4 on programme for ways round this).

There is considerable agreement that a group size of five or six members (large enough for stimulation, small enough for participation and recognition) is the optimum for many purposes, particularly for the more therapeutic person-centred type of short-term closed group. For problem-solving, activity and 'open' groups, larger groups provide more resources and can work well. The tendency to sub-grouping can be used constructively by sub-dividing the group for various tasks and activities. Larger groups usually require more management and structure and are more likely to need two leaders, depending on the extent of leadership among members.

Social work groups often have a drop-out factor both at the stage of group formation (one or two expected members may never actually join the group) and during the group's life. There is also the inevitable temporary absence through illness or other indisposition. For all these reasons, it is desirable to aim for a membership two or three in excess of the required size. This applies particularly in 'closed' short-term groups where replacements may not be possible.

Time-scale

Decisions also need to be taken about the length, frequency and duration of sessions. It is not possible to generalise about these factors as decisions depend on the type of group and its purpose, and may often be negotiated with members anyway. In recent years the tendency in casework to favour brief task-focused intervention has to some extent been paralleled in groupwork with a shift in emphasis from groups that last for years, to ones that are much briefer in duration (say six to twelve sessions over a three- to six-month period), and specific in intent. Groups which *may* require longer time periods include some children's groups, therapy groups, natural groups, support and maintenance groups (e.g. for people suffering from chronic illness) and some groups in residential settings.

Meeting weekly has some advantages over fortnightly, both in keeping up the momentum and facilitating attendance by a regular commitment in the week's arrangements. Flexibility in the use of time for different purposes is, however, essential, and some groups may be most effective meeting intensively over a short period, e.g. several times a week, a whole day or over a block of three days. This block or high frequency approach does not only apply to children's camps and intensive sensitivity marathons, but has also been found to be very effective for example in crisis intervention groups with mental health problems, and in social skills training for the unemployed. This level of commitment will not be practicable for many social workers with heavy workloads, but with careful planning and a flexible team approach, work patterns can be varied. The cultural patterns and life-styles of members are important considerations when deciding the timing of groups, particularly the time of day likely to be most acceptable and convenient, and the optimum length of sessions. See Alissi and Casper (1985) for a series of articles on 'Time as a Factor in Groupwork'.

Open v. closed membership

The dilemma of open versus closed membership faces therapy groups and community action groups alike. Ziller (1965) indicates that the main disadvantages of a changing open membership are possible instability, precariousness and loss of leadership. The main advantages are the potential creativity, flexibility and opportunities for changing a group's culture. A crude guideline is to think of closed membership as rather more likely for short-term groups and planned open membership as more likely to be preferred long-term. Open groups vary from drop-in centres with constantly changing membership, to groups whose membership changes slowly and in a carefully planned way. Schopler and Galinsky (1984) and Galinsky and Schopler (1985) have given special attention to the nature and use of open-ended groups, suggesting practice guidelines, and commenting that 'working with open-ended groups demands a high level of skill, knowledge and flexibility'.

Methods of group selection

The discussion so far has sidestepped the question of *who* makes the decisions about eligibility for, and actual membership of, a group. There is a range of possibilities and clarity about the approach to be used will reduce possible ambiguity, muddle and resentment later.

(*a*) Self-selected groups. These include spontaneously formed 'natural' groups, e.g. peer group in a neighbourhood.
(*b*) Unrestricted membership groups. These include open groups which anyone can join if the aims interest them, e.g. a 'drop-in' centre.

(c) Situationally determined groups. Here, eligibility is decided by descriptive criteria, e.g. being a resident of a hostel, the spouse of an alcoholic, living in a block of flats, being a lone father.

(d) Group-selected. In some open groups, the selection of new members is a matter for the group itself, once it is in existence.

(e) Agency-selected (control by exclusion). In many groups the agency (management, team or groupworker) controls membership by deciding both the descriptive criteria, e.g. isolated women with pre-school children, excluding alcoholics and psychotics, and the specific group composition and size, e.g. 'maximum of ten women, selected to produce a cohesive effective group for the goals of reducing isolation and improving child-care'.

(f) Agency-selected (control by inclusion). In this model, group membership is compulsory and a requirement of some form of statutory supervision or care, e.g. a condition of probation or in-patient psychiatric treatment. Groupworkers and theorists (Roberts and Northen, 1976) differ on the ethics of compulsory group membership, but there is unanimity that the position should be explicit and stated clearly in the group contract.

Leader selection and co-leadership

This aspect of group composition is often neglected in the literature and arrived at quite arbitrarily in practice. Perhaps it is too close for comfort! It will be considered in the chapter on leadership, but is mentioned here as part of group composition because conscious and task-oriented choices of leader need to be made at a very early stage in group preparation.

Prediction of group behaviour

As indicated earlier, some heterogeneity of behavioural attributes is needed in group composition, at least when the aim is some form of change. This requires the groupworker (if she is controlling group selection) to be able to predict how an individual will behave in a small group. Most social workers probably rely on a combination of hunch, previous information about a person (often second-hand from colleagues or records) and an individual interview. How reliable is such a prediction likely to be? Yalom's conclusion after surveying the available research literature is 'of all the prediction methods, the traditional intake individual interview appears the least accurate and yet the most commonly used.' That is not to deny the value of an individual interview as part of the group-composition and contract-making stage, but to indicate its limitations as a predictor of group behaviour. Yalom continues '. . . An individual's group behaviour will vary depending on his internal psychological needs, his manner of expressing them, and the task, interpersonal composition and norms of his social environment.' He then states a general principle: '. . . *the more similar the intake procedure is to the actual group situation, the more accurate will be the prediction of his behaviour'* (Yalom, 1975).

This finding, with its self-evident simplicity, might suggest obtaining information about any previous group behaviour, but this may be un-reliable or non-existent. One approach is to set up some kind of intake or 'suck it and see' group, where in a few sessions, both leader and prospective member can obtain a much more accurate assessment of group functioning and whether it is likely to be the preferred method for that purpose. This approach is already used quite extensively in the USA and in some groupwork programmes in the UK, e.g., intake groups for new probationers, (Brown and Seymour, 1983). An ingenious alter-native, mooted by Yalom, is to show a simulated group situation, say a film or video-recording, to a prospective group member and then ask him questions about his reactions, feelings and identifications with the group and its members. If a film is not available, potential group members can be asked to write down and discuss their feelings about being with other people in groups.

Practical constraints on group composition

The reality of life in most social work agencies means that group com-position is often influenced by factors beyond the individual social worker's control. This calls for a pragmatic approach, but the beginner is recommended to take into account the general guidelines suggested in this section and to resist pressures to take someone who seems quite un-suited to the group. The more experienced groupwork colleague will not necessarily pay less attention to group composition, but one of the skills that grows with experience is an ability to respond flexibly and creatively whatever the group and its composition, including acknow-ledging incompatibility when it arises.

Negotiating a contract

The notion of contract in social work

The contract or 'working agreement' approach to social work

intervention is now widely used. It has two main advantages. One is a philosophy which acknowledges that clients have a right to participate in decisions about their own 'treatment'. The other is a technique which attempts to be more clear and explicit about the aims and methods to be used, and the mutual obligations and expectations of all the participants, including the social worker. A potential disadvantage is inflexibility and unresponsiveness to changing needs. The contract may be written or verbal, the negotiating process itself having as much value as the content. Some literature tends to assume a bilateral worker/client(s) contract, but in statutory agencies a tripartite agency/worker/client concept is needed. The client and worker meet primarily because the agency has functions which it employs workers to carry out, and the client has needs or problems which the agency has a community-sanctioned responsibility to respond to. When several clients are involved, as in groupwork and family therapy, individual contracts, e.g. re goals, have to be reconciled with group or family contracts.

A cardinal rule in contract-making is to be realistic and practical about the level of commitment and achievement which can reasonably be expected of each person.

The contract in groupwork

The main areas to be clarified are:

(a) The aims of the group. What is the group for? (Avoid vague statements.)

(b) Individual goals, consistent with the group aim. What does each individual hope to achieve through group membership?

(c) The methods to be used. Members need to have a general idea of the methods to be used, e.g. discussion, role-play, games, and of any activities that are physically or emotionally demanding and whether participation in them is voluntary.

(d) The practical arrangements of time and place and duration.

(e) Rules, rewards and sanctions (if any), e.g. no violence in the group, early discharge of supervision, outings.

(f) Individual commitments, e.g. to attend regularly, to work at individual goals, to help others.

(g) Confidentiality. In what circumstances, if any, would the leader communicate information about a group member to others in the agency or elsewhere? Is there a group agreement on confidentiality? Are group records or tapes to be accessible to members?

(h) Other social work service. What is the agreement about individual contact with social workers (leaders or others) during the group's life?

(*i*) Agency factors. For members: how does group participation affect any statutory relationship with the agency? For leader(s): what is the agreement with the agency on resources, workload recognition, supervision, insurance and other matters?

Contract negotiability

Different approaches to contract-making offer different levels of negotiating power to the members and leader(s) respectively. Three positions illustrate the continuum of worker–member power: low, medium and high negotiability.

Low negotiability implies a situation where the worker-power is high, and the member-power is low. The group leader(s) makes all the major decisions about the group and the contract content, and the prospective member then decides whether or not to contract in to a largely predetermined package. In a coercive setting, he may be compelled to enter the group on the worker's terms.

Medium negotiability suggests rather more equality: the worker-power and member-power may both be defined as 'medium'. The worker decides initially some broad outline goals and means, perhaps already influenced by clients' ideas, but members have the power to negotiate with her and other members about these and to modify and change them within defined limits, at initial contract-making meetings.

High negotiability implies that worker-power is low, and member-power is high. The worker does little more than provide the resources to enable a group to form and meet. The group membership makes all the major decisions about goals and *modus operandi*. The contract issues to be resolved in this model are mainly between members rather than between member and worker.

The degree of negotiability will vary according to the particular model and philosophy, the aims, the type of membership, the agency expectations and the individual social worker's style. Misunderstandings can arise when it is not clear how decisions are made and who makes them. The 'unforgivable sin' sometimes committed by group leaders is to appear to be very democratic by inviting members' views on everything to do with the group's functioning, and then to exclude them from all the major decisions. When that happens, *actual* negotiability is much lower than *apparent* negotiability, and group members have every right to question the group leader's credibility and integrity.

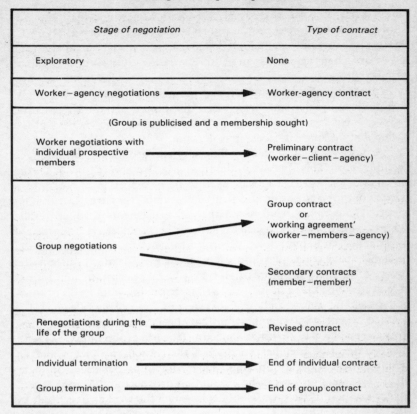

Stage of negotiation	Type of contract
Exploratory	None
Worker – agency negotiations ➡	Worker-agency contract
(Group is publicised and a membership sought)	
Worker negotiations with individual prospective members ➡	Preliminary contract (worker – client – agency)
Group negotiations	Group contract or 'working agreement' (worker – members – agency)
	Secondary contracts (member – member)
Renegotiations during the life of the group ➡	Revised contract
Individual termination ➡	End of individual contract
Group termination ➡	End of group contract

Note: Substitute 'working agreement' for 'contract' if preferred

Fig. 2.1

Contract negotiation stages

The following account of contract stages in formed groups is an elaborated version of that developed by Croxton (1974). The various terms themselves, e.g. 'preliminary contract', will not necessarily be used in practice, but they do represent important processes in the formation of a group in a social work agency. The sequence will vary according to the circumstances (see Fig. 2.1, above).

Having established the need for a group during the exploratory stage, the worker normally has to negotiate with her agency for support and resources before she seeks a membership. This constitutes the *worker – agency contract*. A *draft plan* outlining aims, methods and resource needs will be circulated to relevant individuals as part of the negotiating process. The aim is to obtain agreement with the agency about what they will offer (e.g. consultation, accommodation, transport) and what they expect in return (e.g. general information about the group, effective help for clients). A written agreement is more necessary when there is reason to doubt whether verbal promises will be honoured!

In interdisciplinary settings, such as child guidance or hospitals, negotiations involve staff from other disciplines, e.g. nurses, doctors, psychologists, on whose sanction, if not approval, the viability of the group and the space it needs, may depend.

The next stage is that of publicising the group and attracting a membership. This involves identifying a 'reservoir' of potential members. The basic proposals need to be on paper in the form of a written outline, indicating how firm or negotiable they are. Recruitment methods can range from newspaper advertisements through public posters, agency posters, a general letter or personal letters, to informal approaches and invitations. Recruitment may also be indirect via referrals from colleagues and other agencies. The more distant the source of referral, the more often it may be inappropriate, and special care needs to be taken in such cases (it is surprising what levels of 'misunderstanding' there can be even in referrals from close colleagues!)

Once a potential membership has been identified, the groupworker(s) will usually arrange a meeting (the pre-group interview),with each prospective member to discuss their needs/problems and to explore whether the group might have something beneficial to offer them. Joining a group can be a daunting prospect and Manor (1986) suggests a three-stage process model in which the worker first needs to *engage* with the individual and his personal concerns, then relates these to the group and what it might have to offer (*induction*), and finally has an exchange (*mediation*) about how the person's needs might, or might not, be met in the social context of a group of people with similar concerns and anxieties. This meeting provides an opportunity for questions to be asked about the group and what sort of things are likely to happen when it meets, for groupworker(s) and prospective member to form an initial relationship, and for a mutual assessment to be made of the suitability of the individual for the group and vice versa. Both parties need to know what factors govern the decision to enter into a *preliminary contract* (e.g. does the worker have the power to exclude a prospective member) even if this only commits the individual to attending one or two group sessions in the first instance. Alternatively, more time and a further meeting may be needed. In some instances, significant others are included in the pre-group contract negotiations, e.g. parents and teachers if it is a children's group.

Clients of statutory agencies and others are likely to be ambivalent if not antipathetic to the idea of joining a group. Margot Breton (1985) has contributed an important article on this subject, in which she rejects the notion of the 'unmotivated' person, and challenges group-workers to understand the 'hard-to-reach' stance as having clear motivation based on concern about failure-avoidance, averting risks and maintaining control. If workers are to engage such people in groups they need, she says, to reach out on the other person's terms (and 'turf'!), to demonstrate their own competence in practical ways, to offer challenges pitched at an appropriate level, and to involve natural support networks.

The next contract stage is that of group negotiations, leading to a primary contract or *working agreement*. Most groups start with a contract-making discussion. This is the point at which members can begin to shape the group programme. All the aspects listed above under the contract content need to be discussed, especially the link between individual and group goals. The worker outlines what the group may be able to offer members (emotionally or in activities or skill development) and explains her commitment and that of the agency. This stage can be time-consuming but is vital as a first experience of the leader's role and the decision-making process.

As a result of this negotiation, the prospective member either withdraws or makes a working agreement with the leader(s), the agency and other members. Specific undertakings between members, e.g. on confidentiality, are 'secondary contracts'. A written agreement should include any group rules and sanctions, and have separate sections outlining the respective undertakings of the group member, group leader and the agency. Whilst a written agreement does not suit every group or everyone's style (and is the exception rather than the rule in current practice), it has the advantage over a verbal agreement that it is less open to misunderstanding and confusion. Its disadvantages can be formality, unhelpful pressure and inflexibility. Whether the agreement is written or not, provision needs to be made for contract review and renegotiation as part of a continuous process in which members take a greater share of responsibility for the group.

In closed, short-life groups, the group ends on an agreed date or when the group task is completed (or abandoned). Either way, contract termination at the group and individual level coincides. In an open group, the main criteria for ending an individual's group membership will be task completion as defined in the contract. The process of ending is considered later.

When a social worker negotiates with a natural group, she is an intruder into an existing social system. This makes it essential to define her role and the basis for her intervention, as well as the group members' undertakings to her and to each other. A preliminary contract, e.g. to discuss whether a basis for working together exists, is necessary to start this process.

Motivation and incentives

Many people are not naturally motivated to join groups unless there is some clear gain or benefit to be obtained, although once having joined a group, membership is often experienced as beneficial. An over-all task of the groupworker at the preparation stage is to increase motivation by providing incentives and indicating potential gains from membership. It needs to be attractive, without being gimmicky. Equally, disincentives (e.g. when it is difficult or costly for someone to attend the group), are to be avoided. At the beginning of the life of a group, the worker's enthusiasm is seldom matched by that of the members; by the end it is frequently surpassed by theirs!

Groupwork planning exercise

The following checklist can be used both for training purposes and when preparing for a particular group:

- (*1*) The *need* to be met
- (*2*) The *aim* of the group
- (*3*) The *potential membership?* Who is it for? Who decides on recruitment/referral? Group size? Group composition? Will the group be advertised? If so, how?
- (*4*) The *leadership arrangements?* Who? How many? What roles?
- (*5*) Any particular *theoretical* or *philosophical* basis?
- (*6*) *Methods/techniques* to be used (and how far group programme is decided in advance)
- (*7*) *Group structure*, e.g. open/closed; frequency, timing and length of sessions/activities
- (*8*) *Resources* needed, e.g. time, accommodation, materials, transport, finance
- (*9*) Arrangements for *recording, evaluation, consultation/ supervision*
- (*10*) Do I need anyone's *permission* to start this group?

(*11*) Who do I need to *negotiate* with about this group, e.g. colleagues, bosses, potential members, members' relatives, other agencies?
(*12*) What *obstacles* (to starting a group) are anticipated?
(*13*) What steps/strategies are necessary to overcome the obstacles and create the conditions for starting a group?

Hodge (1977) has produced a more detailed planning outline in his article 'Social Groupwork: rules for establishing the group'.

3. Leaders and Leadership

Leader and *leadership* are two terms that are frequently confused because they are defined and used in many different ways. *Leadership* is a *function* and according to Shaw's definition (1976) is 'a process in which one group member exerts positive influence over other group members'. 'Positive' is used by Shaw in the individual-centred sense of leading the group in the direction that group member chooses, which may not necessarily be towards the group goals. The term leadership will be used here, however, to mean influence which is positive in a group-centred sense, i.e. which helps the group to work at its task, achieve its goals, maintain itself in good working order and adapt to its environment. Leadership may be displayed by any member of a group at any time during the group's life. One way of using the term *leader* is to refer to any group member who is exercising leadership. To try to avoid confusion, we shall use the term *leader* in the specific sense of the person or persons who have a *designated* leadership role, e.g. chairperson, director, consultant, warden, group-worker, facilitator.

In most formed groups in social work, the social worker has some kind of designated leadership role, at least in the early stages. She is seen and behaves as the 'central person' in the group, often being the person who formed the group and to whom more communications are made than anyone else. As the group develops, she may or may not continue to exercise the most leadership. In some models she will gradually move out of the central person role to a position where much of the group leadership is carried by the members. This possibility is often forgotten by anxious group-leaders who feel they must carry all the leadership themselves, in the process denying members *their* potency. Natural groups, like the family or the gang, already have their own leadership structure, and one of the most difficult tasks for the social worker is to establish a viable role for herself which does not undermine the existing structure of the group or the position of the person or persons who are regarded as leaders.

Several theories of leadership are referred to in the literature. The first is the *trait* theory, which assumes that 'leaders are born and not made'. It is now largely discredited as unsupported by research, except for some evidence (Stodgill, 1948) that group leaders do tend to show rather more general ability, sociability and motivation than group members.

The second is the *position* theory of leadership, in which leadership is defined by the formal role or position which an individual holds in an organisation or group.

The third is the notion of leadership as a *style*. The well-known study by Lippitt and White (1953) observed the effects of different leadership styles on activity groups of ten-year-old boys. The three styles, autocratic, democratic and *laissez-faire*, were compared. The principal findings, which have been validated by subsequent studies, indicate that the autocratic approach is at least as effective in task-achievement and productivity as the democratic approach, but produces more dependence and resentment; the democratic approach is much more acceptable, satisfying and creative for the members; and the *laissez-faire* groups are less productive than the others, spending much time discussing their tasks. A simplistic conclusion that a democratic leadership style is always preferable has been superseded by a recognition that it all depends on the particular *situation* and *function* of the group. Interestingly, Shaw's research (1976) indicates that it is easier (though less acceptable to the members) to be an autocratic leader issuing orders, than a democratic leader utilising the abilities of group members effectively.

The fourth theory, developed by Fiedler (1967) is known as the *contingency* model of leadership, linking leadership styles to situational variables. He has shown that when the situation is highly favourable or unfavourable to the leader, a task-oriented style is most effective, but that when it is only moderately favourable, a more relationship-oriented style is required. Highly favourable means high position power, clear goals and methods and good leader–member personal relations. Fiedler's model provides a framework for matching leadership styles and behaviour to the needs of different situations.

Group leadership is concerned with two basic types of leadership, *task leadership* and *group maintenance leadership* (sometimes referred to as instrumental and expressive respectively). *Task-leadership functions* are directly concerned with task achievement and group goals, and include giving information and opinions, seeking

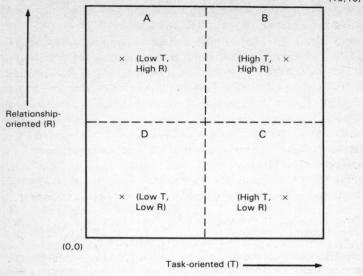

Fig. 3.1

information and opinions, initiating, giving directions, summarising, co-ordinating, diagnosing, clarifying, reality testing and evaluation. *Maintenance-leadership functions* are directed toward the feelings, relationships and participation of the people in the group and include encouraging participation, harmonising and compromising, tension-relieving, helping communication, evaluating the emotional climate, observing processes, setting standards, listening actively, energising, building trust and resolving interpersonal conflict. (These functions, which are based on extensive analysis of how people actually behave in groups, are discussed in more detail in Johnson and Johnson, 1975.)

An effective group requires both types of leadership. Studies show that most individuals tend to be either more task-oriented or more relationship-oriented in their natural style, though some have an even balance between the two. There are some quite simple paper-and-pencil tests (Johnson and Johnson, 1975, Appendix A) for rating your position on a leadership grid. Fig. 3.1 indicates four extreme positions.

A is a relationship-oriented leader, C is a task-oriented leader, B is high on both types of leadership, D is low on both types of leadership. There is no optimum position on the grid because it depends on the type of group and the predominant need. Reddin (1970) suggests a third dimension of effectiveness, which is offering the appropriate leadership style when it is most needed in the group. This raises interesting questions about the leadership-skills repertoire and flexibility of each individual. Some research (Lieberman, Yalom and Miles, 1973) suggests that most individuals *actually* range less widely in their leadership behaviour in different situations than they think they do. T. B. Palmer's research with probation officers in California (1973) indicates that with experience and further training, the social worker can develop new skills and extend her repertoire of behaviour, within certain limits. In casework, limits imply some matching of workers, clients and tasks, but in groupwork there is more flexibility because co-leaders can offer complementary styles, as can group members. Most groups need both task and relationship skills, and if the leader has a bias this can be compensated for by a co-leader or members. (This whole subject of leader-repertoire in groupwork merits further study.)

> *Example*: A social skills group for psychiatric out-patients. The designated leader is leading a role-play on interview technique. He is trying to help one member, Mike, to assert himself in a simulated interview. The leader first demonstrates how to do it himself, and then repeatedly gets Mike to rehearse the behaviour, but little change results. Suddenly, another member, Peter, calls out to Mike, 'Hey, Mike, what's up, you don't seem yourself today?' Mike bursts into tears and tells the group that his friend was killed in a road accident a few days previously. The group members commiserate with him, and the leader suggests he takes a rest while someone else takes a turn at being interviewed. A sensitive group leader might himself have responded to the 'feel' of Mike, but the important thing was that one of the members did so, in the process exercising expressive leadership which enabled Mike to get support and the group to get on with its task.

Authority, power and control

Much that happens in groups revolves around issues of authority, power and control. Social workers in statutory agencies have certain formal authority which derives from their role, professional authority which stems from their training and skill, and personal authority which emanates from their personality. This authority is associated with different kinds of power, classified by French and Raven (1967) as *legitimate* (vested in the role), *attraction* (power from being liked), *coercive* (power to punish), *reward* (power to reward) and *expert* (power of perceived expertise). The designated leader is able to exercise a degree of control over the members because they attribute the authority and power which actually may be quite tenuous. Group members themselves also carry certain kinds of authority and power, and a potential for controlling the leader, other members and the group as a whole. The exercise of power and control may take various forms.

Obvious examples are the leader who tells the group what to do and the member who dominates and tries to take over. Less obvious, but equally potent, is the leader who subtly manipulates the group in the direction she wants, or the member who takes a scapegoat role which preoccupies the rest of the group.

Two anxieties often expressed by social workers leading groups are, paradoxically, discomfort about their authority and fear of losing control. Group members are not helped if the social worker leader 'denies' her authority by behaving exactly as if she was one of them, and not in a different role. There is sameness in person encountering person, but difference in roles and responsibilities. If the leader has not come to terms with her power and authority, she is unlikely to be able to help the members discover and use theirs. The skill lies in functioning as a complete person in a defined role. Authority figures attract other people's projections and strong feelings, which is what makes the acceptance of authority so uncomfortable at times.

The fear of losing control surges up in most group leaders from time to time. What if the group members will not accept what I propose to do? What if there's a dominant person whom I can't control? What if there's total silence? What if two people start fighting? What if I 'fancy' one of the group members? And most frightening of all, what if the group members make it clear that they think the group would do better without me? Most of these fears arise from the false premise that the group belongs to the leader, and she is responsible for all the controlling. Paradoxically, control systems in which the members carry power are likely to be more successful than those which are imposed on them.

Example: A group for people who find it difficult to express their feelings and emotions, with the goal of improving personal relationships. The two leaders decided on a programme which would involve focusing each week on some particular feeling selected by the members, and approaching it by starting off with some experiential exercises linked to the theme, followed by group discussion. The members had accepted this format as part of the initial contract, and followed it with some reluctance for the first four sessions. Then at the beginning of the fifth session one of the members challenged the leaders saying he didn't see any point in doing 'the stupid exercises'. All the members remained silently rooted to their seats, giving passive support. The leaders experienced their own anxiety and anger — *their* plan was being challenged, the whole thing was about to get out of control! After a very tense few minutes, negotiation started, and the planned format was abandoned on the understanding that the members would take their share of responsibility for future planning and process. From that session onwards the group moved forward. A high level of commitment was reflected in one hundred per cent attendance at meetings and a sharing of responsibility for caring, controlling and working at the task. The group was now meeting the members' needs, within the contract, instead of the leaders' pre-planned ideas. The leaders still had important roles and carried authority in the group, but based on legitimate, expert and attraction power, not coercive and reward power.

Lang (1972) has devised a continuum to indicate the different ways in which group control may be shared between leader(s) and members.

```
_____ A _____ B _____ C _____
leader controlled        shared control        member controlled
  (allonomous)        (allon-autonomous)         (autonomous)
```

This continuum can be used in two ways, firstly to locate the pre-dominant position of certain group models, and secondly to indicate movement in the balance of control during the life of a group. For example, in remedial models and many group psychotherapies the worker retains a directive allonomous position (A) throughout, in complete contrast to self-help models which are autonomous right from the beginning (C). In mainstream social groupwork, the worker is often fairly active and directive at the beginning of a new group, functioning initially as the 'central person', position (A), when group patterns are being established, central issues being sorted out, aims agreed and programme negotiated. But then as the group develops and members take on more responsibility, there is a decisive shift to the right and shared control (B). What happens next in the latter stages of a fixed life group depends on the particular model. If the goal is for members gradually to assume responsibility for their own group, then the shift will continue towards the autonomous position (B→C), whereas if the worker retains overall responsibility, there is likely to be a looping back (B→A) as the leader again assumes a more central position to enable her to facilitate the group ending and all that entails.

Leader selection and co-leadership (or co-working)

The means by which a group leader is selected, and a decision reached to have single or co-leadership, is often rather mysterious. Much less attention is given sometimes to leader selection than member selection, with far-reaching consequences for the group. At best, a rational decision is made to select one or more leaders on the basis of particular skills and attributes to meet the group's needs and aims. At worst, an *ad hoc* decision emerges reflecting the personal and political interests of staff and agency, and paying scant attention to group interests. Availability of staff resources is often a constraining factor.

> *Example*: A Family Clinic was planning to run a group for mothers with a linked group for their pre-school children. A newly qualified social worker was keen to establish the group and did most of the preparatory work. It was decided that she and a senior social worker (male) would co-lead the mothers' group, and a child psychologist and health visitor would co-lead the children's group. The clinic was anxious to develop collaboration with health visitor colleagues in this way. Only a week before the group was due to start, the health visitors felt they would like to be directly involved with the mothers' group and a decision was taken to switch the senior social worker and health visitor so the latter would team up with the newly qualified social worker as co-leader of the mothers' group, and the former with the psychologist taking the children. One consequence of this was that the two least experienced workers were taking the mothers, and another was that two female co-leaders were working with an all-female group, who subsequently proved to be particularly preoccupied with their relations with men! This example illustrates in rather an extreme way how agency (and inter-agency) factors can influence leader-selection decisions.

Co-Leadership (or co-working)

Co-leadership has become an integral part of social groupwork practice in Britain (see Brown, Caddick *et al.*, 1982) to the extent that single leadership now tends to be the exception rather than the rule. The reasons for this trend are not altogether clear, but appear to be associated with the struggle to get groupwork established in some agencies, and the perceived benefits of shared working, thinking and support in carrying out what is quite a complex task. As co-leadership is twice as expensive in staff resources (unless the second worker is a student or volunteer) good reasons are needed for having two leaders rather than one, and it is necessary to demonstrate that there are increased benefits for the group members as well as for the workers themselves.

Potential benefits of co-leadership for group members

Most of the potential benefits for group members arise from having two workers with distinctive characteristics who, in combination, can offer the group and each individual more than either would be able to alone. These differences may include:

(*a*) *basic characteristics*: age, gender, race, social background, e.g.

mixed sex groups and racially mixed groups may benefit from having male/female and black/white pairings respectively
(b) *role-difference*: e.g. field social worker, residential worker, health-visitor, youth worker, student, volunteer etc.
(c) *personality/style difference*: e.g. sense of humour, assertiveness, openness, etc.
(d) *differences in preferred mode of communication*: e.g. auditory, visual, kinaesthetic (feelings mode)
(e) *differences in group skills*: e.g. task/maintenance skills, activity/discussion skills, self-disclosure skills etc.
(f) *knowledge/ideas/experience differences*: each worker may bring specialist knowledge and understanding, and will have different life experiences

All these differences offer more choice and resource to the individual member when seeking what he needs, and also an increased chance of finding a worker with whom he feels particular rapport. It should not of course be forgotten that many of these varied attributes and resources will be in the group membership — one of the crucial differences from casework.

The co-workers, as a pair, also offer a model of an interpersonal relationship. The way they relate to each other, for example in managing disagreement, intimacy, conflict, crisis, caring, action, sharing feelings, offering support and so on can provide a helpful model for the members.

Members tend to feel lost in larger groups (8 +) and with two leaders they are likely to get more individual attention and be more noticed.

Benefits of co-leadership for the co-workers

There are several types of potential gain for the workers:
(a) *support*, both in the group, and in negotiating with colleagues and managers
(b) *professional development*: working with a colleague offers special learning opportunities through shared experience, mutual observation and giving and receiving feedback on each other's work performance. The 'apprenticeship model' of student and teacher co-working is a special example of this, although it can turn into a liability if the novice is overwhelmed by the expert
(c) *administrative benefits*: e.g. sharing tasks such as negotiating agency support, obtaining resources, writing letters and records, meeting prospective group members, as well as providing continuity when one worker is ill or on holiday

(*d*) *management and control*: in groups needing active management and control (for example some children's and adolescents' groups) a second pair of hands may be a necessity.

These 'worker benefits' do not in themselves justify co-leadership (the group is created, after all, for the benefit of the members!) but if they indirectly enhance the quality and usefulness of the group for the members, in addition to any direct worker benefits, then they strengthen the case for having two workers. Conversely if the main aim is to protect the workers from stress and exposure, this may not be in the members' interests.

Another factor to be considered is *worker preference*. Some people are much more comfortable working in a pair than alone, others find the sharing irksome and an unnecessary complication. Co-workers form a pair sub-group, which may mean the leader – member relationship is less close than with a single leader.

In summary, it is generally true that the larger, more complex and problematic a group is, the stronger the case for co-leadership. Conversely, the small, relatively straightforward group with highly motivated members willing to take responsibility may be best served by a single worker.

Conditions for successful co-leadership

None of the suggested benefits of co-leadership will be realised unless the two people concerned are able to establish an effective, compatible and trusting work relationship. Co-leadership among incompatibles is a recipe for disaster! It is therefore important to identify what is needed for successful co-working:

(*1*) Both workers need to be satisfied that co-leadership is in the group members' best interests.

(*2*) The two workers need a compatible theoretical and values framework, a shared approach to working with groups and responding to problems that may arise, and some agreement about how active each of them will be in the group. A friendly personal relationship and shared work experience is not, *per se*, a guarantee of successful co-leadership (Paulson *et al.*, 1976).

(*3*) There needs to be a shared understanding about expression of feeling, use of authority and control, and response to conflict, three of the most crucial areas in groupwork practice.

(*4*) The role-relationship needs to be clear. A co-equal model is generally to be preferred, and if there are differences in status and

role in the group, these need to be discussed explicitly, acknowledged, and a different co-leadership model adopted, e.g. leader/
assistant leader, teacher/student etc.

(5) Supervision and/or consultation needs to be available. It is often
very difficult for co-workers to open up with each other areas of
conflict in the work-relationship, and a skilled third person can
facilitate frank dialogue and the resolution of co-working
problems.

(6) Both workers need to be willing to devote considerable time to
preparing themselves as a co-working unit before the first group
meeting.

Co-leadership skills

Before considering leadership skills in general there are some which
apply specifically to the co-leadership model. There are firstly the skills
involved in preparing to work together, secondly, in sharing all the
work done outside the group, and thirdly the in-group co-working
skills.

If the couple are a new pair, some testing needs to be done before the
final decision to work together in a group is confirmed. Opportunities
can be sought to 'practice' working together, perhaps in a training
group or with a relatively straightforward casework task or team
project. Exchanging views about groupwork and ideas about the
proposed group, its members and their needs, is a useful testing
ground. Planning the group together on paper can also be an indicator
of compatibility. Various exercises can be done such as 'draw-a-house'
(two people, with one jointly held pen, drawing their dream-house
together without speaking!), and exchanging the things that you look
forward to and feel apprehensive about when fantasising working with
the other person. After a decision to co-lead has been taken, further co-
working opportunities can be found, including doing some joint
interviewing of prospective group members. Another possibility is
rehearsing the first group meeting with sympathetic colleagues who
offer feedback.

In a co-equals model, the group preparation workload needs to be
shared fairly evenly, and with a clear understanding about who does
what, for instance in liaising and negotiating with management and
colleagues, arranging resources, contacting prospective members and
referrers, doing the written work, negotiating consultancy and so on.

When it comes to in-group co-working skills, there needs to be
agreement about how the different responsibilities and leadership of

particular episodes will be shared. Examples of such tasks are starting and ending the group meeting, introducing particular discussions, activities or exercises, responses at individual and group level, exercising authority, coping with a difficult member and so on. Pairs vary in the extent to which they sharply define in advance what each will do, some preferring a tight structure, and others flexibility. As a rough guideline, more structure may be needed for couples un-accustomed to working together, and at early stages of a group, although some flexibility is necessary to discover how natural styles blend to best advantage.

Co-equal leadership means sharing the responsibility fairly evenly, with neither worker consistently dominating nor deferring to her partner. There needs to be a sensitivity to what your colleague is feeling, experiencing and thinking and an ability to support, but not to overprotect when facing difficulties. Competitiveness and 'splitting' (often provoked by group members) and any wish to appear more able than your colleague, is to be avoided as it can only be unhelpful modelling for the group, if not destructive. A willingness to disagree with, or at least to question your partner in the open group if you sense that what she is doing is not in the group's best interests, can be an asset. Non-verbal skills like use of eye-contact are vital components of the in-group relationship.

A crucial skill of co-leadership is *responding appropriately to the unpredictable happening in the group*. A sudden crisis may occur with someone rushing out, being violent or crying hysterically. Some planned activity may not work or may develop differently from what was expected. In these circumstances, decisions have to be taken 'live' and any consultation can only take place openly in the group. Some-times group members will join in the action and decisions, in a spirit of collective responsibility, and useful learning can result. Much will hinge on the level of trust and mutual confidence between the leaders.

Three person or *multiple* leadership models are often fraught with difficulties arising from confusion about the roles and structure within the staff sub-group. In my view they should only be used when there is an overriding group need for three or more leaders, and when the roles can be clearly defined. An example of this would be an intermediate treatment group of, say, fifteen children, often engaged in activities in several sub-groups and requiring a 5:1 ratio for adequate care and control. There might be one over-all leader and two assistant leaders with clearly distinguished roles.

Readers wishing to study co-leadership further are referred to John Hodge's co-leadership practice guide (1985), to Heap (1985, Chapter 11) and to Galinsky and Schopler's article in a special co-leadership issue of *Social Work with Groups* (1980).

The skills of the group leader

Group-leader skills are more diverse and manifold than those involved when working with an individual. The group leader exercises her skills in four directions. These are leader – member; member – member; leader – group, and leader – external environment. In a co-leadership group there is the fifth direction: leader – leader.

These five directions can be shown diagrammatically for an imaginary four-member group as in Fig. 3.2. The directions can be illustrated by considering one particular skill, communication. The leader needs (a) to establish effective communication, verbal and non-verbal, between herself and each individual group member; (b) to facilitate good communication between members; (c) to be able to communicate with the group as a whole, both at the task and feeling levels; (d) to be able to communicate with all the relevant external persons who can influence the group; and (e) to communicate well with her co-leader, if she has one.

Group-leader skills can be divided into *general skills* and *specific skills*. *General skills* apply to all groups and can be categorised as the

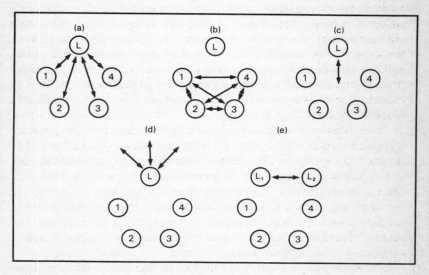

Fig. 3.2

skills of group creation, group maintenance, group task achievement and group culture development. *Specific skills* are those needed for a particular type of group with its specific membership, aims and methods. Examples of specific skills are those associated with outdoor pursuits, activities and games, social skills training, psychodrama and sociodrama, discussion groups, community action groups, TA/ Gestalt, assertiveness training, self-help, arts and crafts, residential group living and behaviour modification. Specialist texts are recommended for detailed consideration of specific skills.

General skills will now be considered in more detail. Firstly, *group-creation skills* which were outlined in the last chapter. They apply only to specially formed groups, but there is an equivalent set of skills which applies to the first stages of work with any 'natural' group. This is the stage of making contact with the group and establishing a valid role and working relationship.

Secondly, there are *group-maintenance skills*. These are the skills associated with the group-maintenance functions listed previously. They involve developing and sustaining these functions over the life of the group. Maintenance skills are not easily articulated because much happens at the feeling level. The worker somehow communicates to the members that she is committed to the group and that she cares very much about each individual in it, and how they are feeling and experiencing group membership. She conveys 'therapeutic optimism', a realistic conviction that the group has the potential to achieve certain things for each member, and that membership can be satisfying and rewarding. The key attributes of empathy, genuineness and non-possessive warmth, identified in casework research by Truax and Carkhuff (1967), apply equally in groupwork. In a group the need is for each member to experience these qualities in the leader. She needs to create opportunities and 'space' for each person to feel sustained, valued and involved.

An over-all maintenance skill is that of mobilising the therapeutic potential and attributes of each member in relation to the others and the shared task. One of the many structured ways of doing this is through co-counselling, when members work together in pairs for a while, each counselling/teaching/supporting the other. Another is when each individual is given space to contribute individually, whether through writing things down, talking in turn, or participating in an activity. How explicit these processes are made will depend on the type of group, but the need will always be there.

The level of trust in a group is a critical factor. Group-maintenance skills are aimed at developing group cohesion and the feeling of security which is a precondition for real trust. Groups often involve members in different kinds of risk-taking, when trust of self and others is put to the test.

The second aspect of group maintenance is sustaining group cohesion, once it is established, and particularly when relationships and individuals in the group are under threat. One way a group can be severely threatened is by erosion of its membership. This is most obvious in a closed group, with no opportunity for bringing in new members. Absent and fluctuating members often breed anxiety and uncertainty in a group, and the maintenance skill involves management of this, either directly or by mobilising the collective responsibility of the group. The skill lies perhaps in communicating and demonstrating that group membership does matter, and carries responsibility. Absenteeism then becomes a cause for concern, rather than for either censure or disinterest. There are technical and ethical dilemmas about when to reach out, e.g. visiting an absent member at home, and when to 'allow' an individual to exercise responsibility for himself in his own way.

Absenteeism is only one of several problematic situations the worker may be faced with. Others involve the behaviour *in the group* of individual members who find themselves in particular roles, e.g. scape-goat, monopoliser, sub-grouper, disrupter, silent member, bore, casualty. The skills and the techniques needed in some of these situations, which depend in part on the worker's theoretical orientation (i.e. individual or group focused) will be described in the final section of the next chapter.

In summary, maintenance skills involve simultaneously responding to individual, interpersonal and group phenomena at the feeling level, thus managing the group process in ways which harness relationships and feelings for task-achievement purposes.

Thirdly, there are *task-achievement skills*. These are skills associated with task-leadership functions. Many such skills are to do with programme development, the subject of the next chapter. Programme is what groups do, and how this is planned to achieve individual and group aims. It involves decisions about structure, planning and imple-mentation. Some groups are much more obviously task-oriented than others, but instrumental skills are needed in all groups. For example, in a group designed to train members in welfare rights and advocacy skills, the task is relatively clear-cut – information is assembled, techniques are discussed and rehearsed. By contrast, a sensitivity or T-group has the task of studying behaviour in the here-and-now, as it happens. There is no planned agenda or activity, but the task is clear, and, *inter alia*, requires the leader to 'gate-keep' (the function of holding to task) if the members try to avoid it by discussing past history or extraneous matters.

A further cluster of task skills involves group assessment and analysis, evaluation, monitoring and recording. These skills are discussed in Chapter 5. There are also the 'external' tasks of the group leader. This includes liaison with relevant persons and organisations, obtaining resources and ensuring optimal external conditions for the group.

Finally, there are *culture-development skills*. 'Once a group is a physical reality, the leader turns his energies to shaping the group into a therapeutic social system. He endeavours to establish a code of behavioural rules, or norms, which will guide the interaction of the group . . . it is the group which is the agent of change.' (Yalom, 1975.)

Group culture is a rather intangible concept, but a very real one. The skill lies in establishing norms and a 'positive' culture via role-modelling and leadership technique. For example, an interactional culture, involving the group as a mutual helping network, may be established by the leader demonstrating at a very early stage that mutual help is to be valued. Instead of answering all questions herself and producing all the ideas, she sets out to reduce this dependence on her as central person. She asks the opinions of different members and invites the group as a whole to answer questions directed at her, encouraging interchanges between members which do not directly involve herself.

A culture of openness, honesty and free expression of feelings can be fostered by the leader being open, honest, sharing *her* feelings, and reinforcing emergent expressions of this in the membership. If the desired culture involved responsible risk-taking (whether rock-climbing, sharing painful feelings or rehearsing a social skill), this behaviour will be modelled by the leader and reinforced in members. Another group cultural factor is respect for boundaries, whether of time, topic or persons. Culture-setting here involves good time-keeping, allowing each person to make his own contribution, and valuing confidentiality and trust.

Group leadership and self-disclosure

The subject of self-disclosure in groupwork and in other social work methods has not received much attention in the literature or on training courses. It is similarly neglected in related professions such as medicine, teaching and nursing. Exceptions are Yalom's helpful discussion of its use (1975, pp. 204–217) and some research into its content by Dies and Cohen (1976). The explanation of the general neglect lies perhaps more in its complexity and threatening nature than its lack of importance. There is evidence (Shulman, 1978; Truax and Carkhuff, 1967) to support the view that the client, user or patient's perception of the professional helper *as a person* has a profound effect on the nature and extent of his participation in 'treatment'.

What are the different kinds of self-disclosure? Firstly, its verbal and non-verbal dimensions can be distinguished. The social worker's general appearance, dress, manner, facial expressions and communicated feelings are a form of self-disclosure just as much as the spoken word. The group members *see* and *feel* the social worker as well as *hearing* her. Secondly, verbal self-disclosure may be the disclosure of personal *feelings*, 'I feel sad', or personal *information*, 'My wife died of cancer'. Thirdly, 'here-and-now' and 'there-and-then' disclosures are quite different in content and impact. The former are usually comments or feelings about the group and individuals in it: 'I feel very alienated from the group today' or 'John, you piss me off when you spoil the football game for everyone else.' There-and-then disclosures mostly refer to past experiences outside the group: 'I was out of work for six months once, so I know a bit what it's like.' Fourthly, there is self-disclosure about one's personal values, beliefs, or ideology: 'I'm against abortion because of my religion, but you must decide what is best for you.'

The aim of self-disclosure, as with any other technique, should be to help group members achieve their personal and group goals. It can be an effective way of role-modelling desired behaviour, e.g. if the group leader expresses anxiety or anger, it is 'OK' for group members to express anxiety or anger; if the group leader shares her personal experience as a parent it is 'OK' for members to do so too. A possible danger in role-modelling is when a comment which shows personal understanding is perceived as apparent endorsement of undesirable behaviour: 'I know what you feel, because when my baby screamed all night I hit him once or twice.' Another quality of self-disclosure is personal authenticity. The group leader who presents as a 'real' person with outside relationships and normal human strengths and frailties, has credibility and is less likely to reinforce members' fantasies about her. This kind of sharing of self is very different from the leader on an ego trip, whose 'performance' and personal revelations may be admired and enjoyed by the members, but which do nothing for their problems and needs.

In contemplating the use of self-disclosure in a group, the practitioner needs to consider the *context*, the *type* of self-disclosure and the *timing*. The *context* refers to the type of group, the model it is based on and its aims. At one extreme is the encounter group whose ethos is maximum personal disclosure and total authenticity. The leader of such a group who discloses nothing of herself will rapidly lose credibility. Conversely, in a positive peer-culture group where the main thrust is within the peer-group, and the leader-role is deliberately circumscribed, extensive self-disclosure would be quite inappropriate.

Regarding the *types* of self-disclosure outlined above, the Dies and Cohen research indicated that there-and-then disclosures are generally experienced as less threatening than here-and-now revelations, particularly when the latter involves negative feedback to individuals as distinct from general expressions of feeling about the self or the group.

Timing is very important. Extensive use of self-disclosure in the early stages of a group is not helpful, particularly expressions of self-doubt about the group. At that stage the members are usually looking to the leader as a reliable strong person who shows conviction about what she is doing, and who can cope. They are not, however, seeking a superwoman or superman and some relatively non-threatening disclosure of personal vulnerability at an early stage can be reassuring. An example of this was a first meeting of a men's group. There was a tense silence and an awkwardness when the first session was due to begin. The leader said he expected everyone was feeling rather anxious as he certainly was. This had the immediate effect of relaxing the tension in the group, shown by the taking off of jackets and more relaxed postures. The leader had role-modelled 'it's OK to be anxious'.

Once the group is well established as a cohesive unit with leadership being shared by the members, more personal forms of leader self-disclosure may be risked, provided these are primarily for the benefit of the members and not the leader. For example, an intermediate treatment group, which has been running for several months, goes away for a week's camp. At the camp the context is different, it becomes a group-living situation (as in residential work), the group is well established and it may be very important for the children to experience their social workers as 'real' people with normal human foibles. Many social workers speak of the deeper relationships and trust which develop from this kind of exposure and mutual encounter as 'real' people.

Finally, self-disclosure is not just a matter of learned techniques. It depends on the social worker's feelings about herself as she actually is, and her confidence in using all the parts of herself in her work. For some people this state comes naturally, but for many it requires training and structured experiences in group membership.

4. Group Programme and Group Process

This chapter is concerned with what happens in groups, and how this can be influenced by programme. All groups have natural processes or group dynamics, and the skill of the groupworker lies in developing a programme of activities which phase in with the stages and condition of the group, to provide the best possible opportunities for task achievement. The term 'activities' is used here in the broadest sense, to describe anything which a group may be engaged in from talking together, to playing games, to meeting with a local authority official. Each group model influences the choice of activities, as does any working agreement about aims and methods. Our general assumption, however, is that groupworkers need to be flexible and pragmatic in their use of programme, drawing on different sources and ideas.

The following sections will discuss the concept of programme, and the general considerations and questions which arise; the natural process of groups, and the stages of development which they may follow; the range of activities available for programme planning, and some of their possible uses; and, finally, some indications of programme technique which can be used to help manage problematic situations, including scapegoating and 'stuck' groups.

Programme – the concept and some general considerations

Programme as a concept and working tool is not prominent in the groupwork literature (but see Middleman, 1980; Heap, 1979; Briscoe, 1978). This may be because it tends to be equated with a structured goal-oriented approach. In reality, every group has a programme if we define it as *what the group does as a means of trying to achieve its aims*. With this definition, a decision to run a group on an existential creative spontaneity basis is as much a programme decision as is an elaborate timetable of visits, talks and structured activities. There is a distinction to be made between *potential* or *planned* programme and *actual* programme. The former is what is planned in advance, the latter is what the group actually does, and the two do not always approximate!

Some basic considerations affect decisions about programme. The first two are philosophical as well as technical.

(a) Structure and spontaneity. Every group has to reach some balance between pre-arranged structure and spontaneous development. Some groups are so pre-planned and rigid that there is no scope for response to the needs of individual members and their unique group. Others are so vague and unstructured that they drift along aimlessly, without anyone really knowing what they are there for, or what they are supposed to be doing. Groups need both the security of some known structure, and the flexibility necessary for learning and change.

(b) Person and task. Every group is concerned with its members as people, and with the tasks for which it is met. A group with person-centred aims, as in group psychotherapy, is likely to devise a person-centred programme. A group which is highly task-oriented, whether that task is located at the individual, group or community level, is likely to devise a programme emphasising procedures, decisions and the monitoring of task achievement. Most social work groups require a sensitive balance between focus on persons and focus on task. This is one reason why programming is a highly skilled aspect of groupwork.

(c) Individual factors. Programme depends on what the members are capable of, and this varies according to age, verbal ability, practical ability, motivation and self-control. In groups with a wide ability range, programme needs to include activities adaptable to individual differences.

(d) Group factors. Programme takes into account fixed factors such as group composition and size, and variable factors associated with the stage of development the group has reached, and its current state. This includes group morale, cohesion, conflict and the level of commitment to task.

(e) The individual and the group. Programme should be consistent with what has been agreed with individuals and the group in the initial contract, although as a group develops, needs and interests change, and opportunities for renegotiating programme should be available.

Programme involves a blending of activities which include the whole group with those which individuals undertake on their own, or in pairs, or sub-groups. As a guideline, individual and pairs activities may be more needed in the early stages, when group experience is rather daunting for some members.

(*f*)   Resources. Many activities need resources, both cash and kind. This may be a real limitation on programme, and it is unethical to raise members' expectations about exciting activities unless necessary resources will be available.

Given these basic considerations, the groupworker then faces a number of questions.

What will the group actually do?

Traditionally, groupwork has relied heavily on the use of discussion and a limited range of other activities. A much wider range of possibilities is now available (as will be seen later in this chapter) and this is constantly being added to by the creativity of group leaders and members. The choice within this range is dependent not only on the task, resources and member capabilities, but also on the skills and capability of the leader. Group members are quick to sense whether a group leader feels comfortable with the methods she is using, and if she reveals excessive anxiety and uncertainty it will be rapidly transmitted to others. It may make them reluctant to engage in the activity, and more vulnerable to failure. Groupworkers wishing to extend their repertoire of activities and skills by trying out a new approach for the first time, can usually do so with more confidence if they have rehearsed it beforehand in the relatively 'safe' setting of the team or a training session, perhaps using video playback.

Who makes programme decisions and how are they made?

The agency, the leader and the group members all play a part in programme decisions. Agency influence is exerted through general policy and control of resources. Within these constraints, decisions depend on negotiations between leaders and members. A combination of leader anxiety and member dependency sometimes results in a leader-selected programme in the early stages. This may be helpful initially, but there is the danger of establishing a dependency pattern in which members' own ideas and wishes are not valued. If a leader opts for an approach which offers members a significant say in what the programme will be, a group decision-making process becomes necessary. The management of this requires considerable skill as the leader balances group aims and her own ideas and wishes with those of other group members which may diverge. Both leader and members need to be clear about *which decisions are negotiable and how any conflicts will be resolved.*

A simple example of this is seen in the programme decision about when group meetings will be held. At one group this was to be decided at the initial contract-making meeting. The two leaders knew which evenings they would prefer, Friday not being one of them. When it came to deciding, one of the group members took it upon himself to organise a vote to see which evening was the most popular. Friday won the vote and the leaders had to rearrange personal programmes to accommodate it. Their first 'mistake' was not making it clear that certain evenings were not negotiable, the second was not questioning voting as a means of making decisions, there having been no group agreement to use voting in this way. They were confused about the nature of their authority in that group, and how much power they could or indeed wanted to wield. On the positive side, the members got an early message that contract-making was a genuine process in which their interests counted.

In group decision-making processes, the more reticent members can be dominated by the more assertive and articulate. The leader may need to devise methods which allow each individual to express his views freely, and to ensure that those views are given equal consideration.

How much is planned in advance?

Some activities require much more forward-planning than others. A week's camp, a meeting with the local police inspector or an invitation to another group for a meal, all need varying degrees of advance preparation. So does the use of video, as the equipment has to be obtained, set up and checked. A trust exercise, role-play or walk needs less pre-planning, although the leader herself still needs to be adequately prepared.

These are the practicalities of planning ahead, but which activities and approaches are best suited for different stages of the group's life? To assess this, an understanding of how groups develop and change over a period of time is needed.

Group processes and stages of development

Group process has been defined by Garvin (1974) as 'those changes occurring in the activities and interactions of group members that are related to changes in goal attainment and group-maintenance'. One of the most profound characteristics of group process is the way in which the whole mood and functioning of a group, the roles, behaviour, communication patterns and interaction of the members can and do change quite dramatically over a period of time. These changes have been studied by researchers (Sarri and Galinsky, 1974; Garland, Jones and Kolodny, 1965; Schutz, 1958; Tuckman, 1965) who have identified the typical stages of development of most groups. Hartford (1971) includes the *pre-group stage*, sub-divided into 'private' (someone has the idea) and 'public' (active promotion of a group) phases. There are *linear* models of group development in which one stage follows the next progressively, *cyclical* models, and *helical* versions which combine linear and cyclical tendencies in a spiralling concept. Whilst the linear approach is an over-simplification (every group has setbacks and periods of regression) it is a useful starting-point, and we shall therefore use Tuckman's stages of *forming, storming, norming* and *performing* with the addition of the final stage of *ending*, or if you prefer the rhyme, *mourning*! Each of these stages will now be discussed in turn, indicating their significance at both the group's maintenance and task/activity levels, and what this suggests for worker behaviour and programme.

Forming

This is the stage when the group first starts. Initially, it is a collection of individuals, each of whom will be preoccupied with issues to do with *joining* or *inclusion*. They will be drawing on their past experience of other groups, searching for similarities and looking round for other individuals with whom they may feel some affinity (isn't that what *you* do when you join a new group?). At the emotional level, behaviour is often characterised by approach-avoidance movements as new members 'dip their toes in the water' tentatively exploring the group's attractiveness and the limits on what they personally can do. There is often much dependence on the leader and an apparent willingness to conform to whatever is suggested. Sometimes an extrovert individual is very active and talkative, making a successful but often temporary bid for the leadership. Another member may start by pouring out personal problems or views before he or the group is ready to deal with them. At the task level, there may be reluctance by members to take responsibility for helping to plan the programme and decide on individual and group goals. Discussion may ramble and become anecdotal. These behaviours are quite common in the initial stages of many groups, but are likely to be more pronounced when members have not been in a formed group before. The groupworker can easily underestimate the anxiety this new experience can produce for the individual who has not yet learned *how to function in the role of group member*. It takes time and experience to discover how you as a member can use a group to benefit yourself and other members.

The forming stage will be affected by whether the group is a 'stranger' group (in which all start from the same base line) or a group in which some or all the members already know each other, whether through previous agency contact – perhaps another group – living in the same neighbourhood, being part of the same family or social network or for any other reason. This introduces a 'past history' into the group which will inevitably affect role-expectations and group behaviour, not least if some members have had an individual work-relationship with the worker and others have not. Some of these previous relationships will not only be obvious, but will be openly declared, perhaps in the form of sub-groupings, cliques or a member claiming a special relationship with the worker. Others will be hidden, perhaps because of embarrassment (as in one group when one member found herself sitting next to another who was the childminder for her children and knew details of her personal life – she later withdrew), antipathy or uncertainty. Secret relationships within a group are at best constraining and at worst destructive, and it is therefore desirable, as a general guideline, to encourage the open acknowledgement of these relationships at an early stage in the group's life. There will, however, be occasions when for reasons of confidentiality, privacy or at a member's request it is not appropriate to encourage disclosure. The skill of the worker lies in using the 'sociometry' of the group as a positive force for group-development and task-achievement. The initial programme can be arranged, for example, with the deliberate choice of activities in which members work in stranger pairs or sub-groupings for a while. Sub-groupings can promote a positive basis for group cohesion if that energy contributes to the group as a whole and is not encapsulated or split off. The worker also needs to demonstrate verbally and non-verbally that she is equally concerned with all members, whether or not she knew some of them before.

Another possibility is that everyone in a 'new' group already knows each other, as may happen in a residential setting, or an institutional setting such as a prison, a school or a social work training course. In these settings the task of the leader at the forming stage is concerned with a more complicated joining process. She needs to establish a clear purpose and boundary for the group, separating it, but not isolating it, from the normal life of the institution. This can be facilitated by careful choice of location, and by a task and programme which is manifestly different from other things done outside the group. The members will need help in freeing themselves from expected roles and behaviour patterns, and in using their group experience and learning in the rest of the group-living experience. If the leader is a member of staff in the establishment, there will be dual-role problems, particularly if she is in some formal authority role. This should be openly acknowledged. In the residential setting, the programme of any specific group should be seen as part of an integrated twenty-four hour programme for the whole establishment, with staff working as a team, supporting one another in the different roles they carry. If the staff can collaborate across these boundaries whilst still maintaining them, then the residents have a chance of 'mirroring' their behaviour and doing likewise.

The groupworker's task at the first meeting of a new group has several basic components, the emphasis and chronological order varying according to the type of group:

(*1*) To facilitate introductions and help the members to join together to form a group which is attractive to them and to which they feel some commitment. This may be done by the use of some suitable structures and exercises (see next section) which involve members from the beginning in active participation with each other, and as a group.

(*2*) To make a clear statement about why the group has been formed, and how its purpose is viewed by the workers and the agency, allowing space and time for the members to respond and express their views.

(*3*) To 'clear expectations' with members about why they have come, what they would like to do and what they are hoping to gain from the group.

(*4*) To negotiate and agree the group contract (see Chapter 2), including the way in which members will work together and any group 'rules'. If attendance is non-voluntary, the implications of this need to be clear.

(*5*) To discuss the group programme, methods to be used and to consider what will happen at the next meeting.

(*6*) To indicate the way the worker(s) hopes to work with the group and what her role will be.

(*7*) To begin to establish group culture, for example the philosophy of a mutual aid system and shared responsibility.

In some groups, some of these aspects will only be touched upon at a first meeting. For a lucid account of worker skills in the beginning stage of a group, see Shulman (1984, Chapters 9 and 10).

Another variation on 'forming' is the re-forming which is necessary when a new member joins an already existing group. Anyone who has experienced this when taking a new post in an existing work-team will know how difficult the joining can be, and how important the initial reactions of the group are. There is the 'ghost' of any person who has been replaced to contend with, plus the culture and past history of the group before you joined it. The new member's feelings are likely to include both a wish for recognition and a fear of early exposure in a new culture. This anxiety may show in a low profile or an assertion of self ('You've got to notice me'). The programme should include advance preparation of the group and the newcomer for the change. In some groups the members contribute to the decision about a new person joining and they are likely to be more receptive if they feel the newcomer has not been imposed on them. An introduction and procedures which establish the newcomer as a group member in the re-formed group whilst allowing him to ease his way in gradually, can be helpful. Galinsky and Schopler (1985) have researched the patterns of entry and exit in open groups and identified useful guidelines for practitioners.

Storming (and depression?)

This is a critical stage in the group's development, and it can be make-or-break. It is the point at which members are beginning to seek individual roles and space, and conflict can arise as they jockey for position and search for compatible roles within the group. Issues of control and power are prominent, and these may be tested in leader—member as well as member—member interactions. Anyone who feels he has been coerced into the group is likely to reveal this in some way. For some members, or even for the group as a whole, the 'fight' may turn inward and show as depression or 'flight'. Members often arrive at a new group with unrealistically high expectations, and a depressed feeling after a few sessions can result from the realisation that the group offers no magical solutions to problems, but that any gain is likely to involve personal investment and effort.

After initial fears of not belonging, the opposite fear of group absorption and loss of individual significance may surface. Personal needs and aspirations have to be compromised if a culture of sharing is to develop in which each member's needs are to be expressed and met.

The leader is likely to experience conflicting messages of both dependence ('Please lead us through this confusion and control us') and independence ('This is our group now, and we intend to challenge your leadership and power').

At the task level, there may be anxiety and uncertainty about what individuals can achieve and how the group can help them. It is therefore very important that all members get involved in group activity, and experience some initial success and progress at this stage. This suggests activities which are relatively non-threatening, undemanding and well within the capabilities of members. If the group is stuck in verbal deadlock, a change of emphasis may be needed to involve members in other ways, perhaps through games and simulations or some of the easier drama therapy techniques. 'Positive feedback' from self, fellow members and leader provides the necessary reinforcement and encouragement to continue. This applies equally to a psychotherapeutic group, a social skills group or a community group, e.g. when a recently formed tenants' group is facing political pressure from a powerful housing department, it is crucial that initial tasks are manageable and have a good expectation of success. Ambitious, unrealistic goals, such as changing a policy overnight, can only result in disillusionment and quite possibly the demise of the group.

The group is still quite fragile, and the leader may need to demonstrate security by controlling individual members if they test the limits. This requires a firm but sensitive approach aimed at reducing unhelpful conflict. P. B. Smith (1978) suggests that the leader needs to seek an appropriate balance between confrontation and support, avoiding any polarisation of these two approaches.

The 'storming' stage can be rather difficult for the novice leader, particularly if the members are inexperienced too, and an experienced co-leader and/or supervision and support are necessary. The more experienced leader is also likely to be anxious but she develops a time perspective which reminds her that this often happens in groups, and that if she remains relatively calm and optimistic, this should help the members. Similarly, the experienced group member can be a great help to a leader, communicating a realistic confidence that the group will develop and members will begin to achieve some of the things they joined for.

Note Suggestions about ways of responding to the kinds of difficulties that may arise at this stage are discussed later on in this chapter.

Norming

When the group has successfully sorted out some of the issues of power and control, it is freed to develop trust, cohesion and a degree of intimacy. The group begins to be important to the members, relationships matter, and emotional investment in 'our group' develops. Group culture emerges. Part of this process is the establishment of norms, or accepted ways of doing things, and agreement about sanctions and where the limits are.

At the emotional level, individuals may start sharing more of themselves, and if conflicts arise they may be in the area of personal relationships and attractions. The stability which is established may be at the cost of one or more members carrying 'scapegoat' roles, and if this causes the leader to feel the need to challenge the apparent harmony, she is likely to be unpopular. This is because a feature at this stage is a tendency for the group to become an end in itself for the members. The leader's aim is to try to harness this group togetherness and cohesion for task achievement. One way of doing this is by steadily increasing the members' participation and investment in programme decisions and implementation.

The point at which group members begin to take responsibility, individually and corporately, for the group and its tasks, is the point when they are ready to 'perform'. This stage is often a watershed or breakthrough in a group's success. For the leader, it is like having a weight lifted from her shoulders. Programme design can now encourage the taking of risks in the direction of change. In a Gestalt group this might mean taking the 'hot seat' and working at difficult painful areas of personal development. In a positive peer-culture group it could mean confronting a peer-leader if he is deviating from acceptable behaviour. In a social skills group it could mean agreeing to test interviewee skills in a real interview. In a community group it could mean chairing an important meeting for the first time, or having a dialogue with a councillor on the radio. In a residential group it could mean behaving in ways which risk a comeback from others outside the group. In a single parent group it could mean sharing feelings about sexual deprivation.

Some models refer to a 'revision stage' or cyclical effect when a group has a set-back, or crisis of some kind. This could be at the emotional level, as when one member's behaviour causes others to seek to remove him from the group, or at the task level, if an individual or group project fails. These occasions can be used by a leader and the group as opportunities for reviewing progress and reassessing the programme. A stock-taking session can be very productive, and serve as a springboard for the next move forward.

Programme design during the life of a group should stress increasingly the links between what members do in the group and their functioning in the 'real world'. One effective way of doing this is the use of *assignments* or homework, in which members accept achievable tasks to work at or try out *between* sessions, perhaps with support from other group members, with agreement to report back to the next meeting. This emphasises that the group is a means to an end, and not (in most cases) an end in itself. A danger, to be avoided if possible, is allocating tasks which put too much pressure on individuals, bringing fear of failure, and sometimes making it difficult for them to come to the group any more.

Performing

Much performing occurs at the norming stage, and the distinction is one of emphasis only. Performing is the point at which the group becomes a largely self-sufficient resource, using all the skills and potential of the members to achieve its aims and solve problems. It is likely to have an enabling structure and a high level of cohesion and trust. In some groups, e.g. self-help, mutual support, or community based, this may be the point at which the group becomes autonomous and takes on its own identity, independent of the social workers and the agency. It may serve as a model for other groups to learn from and emulate. Many groups (particularly short-life groups) do not reach this stage.

Ending

Most groups come to an end. Many have a fixed time span, known from the beginning, others end when the task is completed or when there seems no purpose in continuation. Some are continuous but with changing membership, so they have individual endings, but not a group ending.

We shall first consider group endings. These are characterised by various predictable feelings and behaviour. Frequently group members want to postpone the ending by continuing beyond the agreed date. There is a belief that if only there were more time, all the goals could be achieved. A modified version of this is a wish to have periodic 'reunions'. These pressures are quite seductive because they may have some validity, but leaders should be cautious when considering negotiating an extension (often only some members really want it, and then attendance may be poor and motivation lacking). There may be euphoria that much has been achieved, or the opposite extreme, a discounting of achievements. There is sometimes depression about the loss of 'what might have been' and sadness at the ending of the group and the personal relationships.

The leader has several programme responsibilities connected with group ending. The first is to make it clear from the beginning that the group has a limited life (if it has), and periodically to remind members of this as the group develops. Secondly, she needs to help members to link group activities and experience to their outside 'real' world and to do this increasingly as the group approaches its end. Thirdly, she needs to help members to evaluate realistically what they and the group have achieved and have failed to achieve. This process should be started some time before the final session, so members have a period of mental preparation and adjustment. There may be tangible evidence to draw on, such as something they have made, improved school attendance, travelling on a bus (for an agoraphobic) or obtaining a job. Fourthly, there may be 'unfinished business', perhaps between members, or members and leader. It is important to create opportunities (e.g. feedback exercises) for this to be acknowledged, and if possible resolved, before the group disperses, or an individual leaves. Fifthly, individual members need assistance in planning continuation and consolidation of development and achievement after the group ends. This involves working out ways of replacing the group by other community support systems. These may include other group members, family, volunteers, clubs, other groups, social work help and so on. The whole emphasis is on the group not being an isolated experience for the individual, but a process which is linked to their social functioning.

Groups often suggest some kind of ritual ending such as a party, a trip or an evening in the pub. As with other rituals which are concerned with role-transition, this can be very useful as a visible ending and marking of the boundary between group and no group.

Group endings are often quite difficult for the leader because she too feels the emotion and sadness (sometimes accompanied by relief which she may feel guilty about!). A good way to deal with this is by openly acknowledging it in the group. The leader role-models 'it's OK to be sad'.

The powerful influence of group atmosphere is never more evident than at the time of ending. Programme can help by ensuring that every individual has the space and time to disengage from each of the other members and the leader.

When a group ends prematurely because of 'failure' (e.g. lack of members, task not achieved, no more funds), the leader has a special responsibility to try to help members cope with the mixture of feelings of anger, sadness, relief and frustration, at the same time as struggling with her own disappointment. She, in turn, will need support from colleagues and supervisor.

Individual endings in a continuing group are obviously much easier when the reason is goal achievement than when it is some kind of failure or incompatibility. The programme skill lies in making space for the individual to evaluate his progress (including feedback from other members), and disengage emotionally from the group, whilst the group's work for the remaining members continues. One device for doing this is to establish a leaving ritual which every member has a right to. In some groups, especially those with a peer-culture emphasis, the decision about individual withdrawal is viewed as a matter for the group as a whole, just as individual joining of a continuous group may be a group decision. This model has the advantage of a built-in disengagement process. As with other group phenomena, one individual's leaving predicament resonates for others, motivating them to think about their membership and progress. This can be both unsettling and productive.

Two general points need to be made about the Tuckman and other models of group stages. The first is that to a degree the same series of stages are experienced at every group meeting, as well as over a series. Each time a group reconvenes there will to some extent be a reforming, an adjustment, an acknowledgement of the 'rules of the game', a period of 'work', an evaluation and an ending. The second point is a word of caution. All groups are different, and the phases of development will depend, *inter alia*, on 'the particular needs of members, the type of setting in which they meet and the orientation of the leader in that group' (P. B. Smith, 1978). There is *no* suggestion that every group follows the above stages in a neat progression. Tuckman's model, Schutz's 'inclusion, control and affection' cyclical model (1958) and others are extrapolated from studies of groups in general, and merely offer guidelines. Stages always overlap, and the intermediate ones follow no clear sequence. What can safely be said is that most groups have beginnings, middles and ends, that characteristic behaviours are associated with each of these stages, and that programme planning and activities must take account of these characteristics. There will also be variations as between stranger and non-stranger groups, open and closed groups and field and residential settings. The reader who wishes to study another model is encouraged to read Garland, Jones and Kolodny (1965), who in addition to describing and illustrating the stages of development in their children's groups, also discuss conceptual and practice issues.

Group activities and techniques

Vinter (Glasser, Sarri and Vinter, 1974, Chapter 13) suggests that group activities can be analysed into six general factors.

(*a*) Prescriptiveness. Activities vary in the extent to which they prescribe an individual's behaviour (e.g. open discussion is low in prescriptiveness, but a game of badminton is high).

(*b*) Controls. The sources of control vary between the individual, other group members, the leader and the rules (e.g. football has its rules and the control of the referee; psychodrama has the control of the dramatherapist; an unstructured swimming session relies heavily on individual self-control; a guided group interaction session places control mainly with the peer group, but with the leader as back-up).

(*c*) Physical movement is central to some activities (e.g. bioenergetic exercises), and peripheral to others (e.g. a discussion group).

(*d*) Competence and skill. The demands on a group member's ability can be varied by choice of activity (e.g. rock-climbing, clay modelling, trust exercises), and within the range of a particular activity (e.g. climbing a simple practice rock, negotiating a severe overhang).

(*e*) Participant interaction. Activities vary from those which are individualistic (e.g. writing your own ideas down on a piece of paper), to those which require maximum group interaction (e.g. a sociodrama re-enactment of a court scene).

(*f*) Reward structure. Activities have their pains and pleasures. They can be rewarding tangibly ('I made that cake'), or less tangibly ('I feel really good after our group-meeting').

Davies (1975) mentions a seventh factor, to do with the *degree of creativity*: e.g. a role-play with scripted roles is more limiting on creativity than a guided group fantasy in which anything (or almost anything!) goes.

With Vinter's general factors in mind, we shall now describe the range of group activities and techniques.

Name-learning techniques

In any stranger group, name-learning is a top priority in the joining process, and it is often accompanied by some brief information about the person, if they wish to divulge it. In a group larger than six, the conventional approach of asking each person in turn can be quite threatening, and also a fairly ineffective way of learning. Variations include starting off in pairs, exchanging names and brief information, and then introducing each other to the group; going round the circle naming yourself and your neighbours; or finding your name pinned on someone else's back. One very effective method is playing catch with a soft object and calling the name of the person you throw it to, culminating in each person going right round the circle. This can be done sitting down, or moving around. The leader's participation and role-modelling is important, as is her sensitivity to the approach likely to work best with a particular group.

Trust exercises

These are used particularly in the early stages of some person-centred groups, but may be used at any time. Some are done in pairs, e.g. falling backwards and a partner catching you, and the 'blind-walk' in which one person leads another blind-fold, without talking, for five or ten minutes, and then roles are reversed. Other trust exercises involve the whole group together, as when the group forms a close circle and an individual member stands in the centre, eyes closed, and is supported as he sways to and fro in a gradually widening circle. It is important to allow time for expression of feeling and discussion after each exercise or sequence of exercises. Groupworkers need to be comfortable themselves about doing these kind of exercises, sensitive to members' feelings about doing them, and there needs to be an explicit understanding that participation is voluntary. Some people find any form of physical touch extremely threatening and are likely to prefer to explore trust in other ways. Many examples of trust exercises are described in Brandes and Phillips (1978) and Ernst and Goodison (1982).

Talking

There are many variations on talking in a group. The *co-counselling* or *tandem* method, when members work for a while in pairs, can be very productive, and in larger groups offers a welcome time of personal attention, a form of refuge from group pressures. This pairing can either be very prescriptive ('One of you speak to the other for two minutes about things you do well, and then reverse roles for two minutes'), or more open ('Share with each other how you feel about yourself and the group today'). The issue of selection of a partner for any paired activity in a group is a sensitive one and can be either random, freely chosen or chosen according to some criterion. Random methods may be less threatening in the early stages. When numbers are odd, the leader must judge whether one threesome or a pairing with herself would be most appropriate. Co-leaders can model co-counselling with each other, or observe the members.

At group level the variations revolve around structure and aims. Discussion can be either completely unstructured (you speak when you feel like it), or structured so that each individual has a turn, or some blend of the two. Periodic structure to give each individual space can be productive and also an effective way of avoiding confronting 'silent' members, who often find some structure a supportive way of getting involved. Discussion in sub-groups is another variation.

The leader needs to learn the natural language and communication styles of the members, as a background to the programme. Conversely, certain activities and therapeutic models have a language which members need to learn and use, e.g. in a rock-climbing group technical terms such as belay and absail; in a TA group key words and phrases such as critical parent, scripts, stroking, adapted child, stamp-collection and 'not OK'. In positive peer-culture groups, members learn a vernacular of problems such as 'low self-image', 'inconsiderate of others', 'authority problem' and 'fronting'. These models are distinguished from traditional psychotherapy and behaviour modification which also have their language (e.g. counter-transference, desensitisation), but it is usually reserved for the therapists.

Writing

This is a very important activity in a group. It can be used by members at the individual level for self-positioning, self-assessment and goal-setting; periodic evaluation, reflection and ideas; and personal recording. Blank sheets can be used accompanied by verbal guidelines, or written instructions used for sentence completion, questionnaires, scales, check-lists, or the snakes and ladders of personal history and aspirations. Many of these exercises are described by Priestley *et al.* in *Social Skills and Personal Problem Solving* (1978). Writing can also be a group activity, using a blackboard or large sheets of plain paper and felt-pens. The purpose may be brainstorming (aimed at producing a large number of ideas on a chosen topic), constructing a group contract and programme, planning a meeting or trip, making a recipe, etc.

Periodic individual or group writing sessions have value as a variation on discussion, and can be used to obtain a change in tempo or emphasis. Writing creates time and space for people to express their thoughts and feelings in a different way. A disadvantage is that some people are either illiterate or find writing very difficult. Leaders must be sensitive to this, but should not underestimate what each individual can achieve, with help from them and other members.

Refreshments, cooking, eating and drinking

If refreshments or a meal are to be part of the programme, the timing, arrangements and content are important. Some groups have refreshments either before or after the group session, and they may thereby signify the social/work time boundary. Others, particularly children's groups and half-day or longer groups, use refreshments during the proceedings, perhaps to separate different activities, or to build in a period of relaxation and informal interchange. Providing refreshments is also a direct and valuable form of caring. As the group develops, members themselves often like to share responsibility for the preparation.

Learning how to cook may be a programme activity with both therapeutic and skill-development elements. A female probation officer ran a very successful 'pie-making' group for male offenders in their late teens. Although quite tough and sophisticated in crime, they committed themselves enthusiastically to weekly pie-making sessions, becoming proficient at the skills, but also sharing themselves and their problems with each other and the probation officer in the process. Walker (1978) in her lucid account of a Family Service Unit parents' group describes how an invitation to eat a meal prepared by a rival FSU group stimulated her group to include planning and preparation of lunch as a central feature of their programme. Walker points out how cooking meals together developed individual skills, social interaction and a capacity to plan ahead.

Social skills techniques

Groups provide a supportive forum for developing social skills. There is the opportunity for *role-play* and *rehearsal* of skills including interview technique, assertiveness training, handling frustration, saying 'no', managing personal relationships, interacting at a party, coping with the boss, and many others. Everyone has skills to develop, and there are roles for other group members in the role-plays and offering feedback. The various techniques are described in detail in Priestley *et al.* (1978), McGuire and Priestley (1981) and Bond (1986).

Psychodrama

Psychodrama is one of several drama-based techniques which use live enactment of personal or social experiences. It has much to offer groupworkers, and Blatner's *Acting-In* (1973) gives a clear exposition of 'practical applications of psychodramatic methods'. In psychodrama the individual is helped to enact his problem instead of just talking about it. The emphasis on non-verbal communication, movement and experience makes it a particularly effective medium for children, the mentally handicapped, the inarticulate, the over-intellectualisers and some categories of offenders and psychiatric patients. The structured group experience provides the context for enactment designed to turn acting-out impulses into insights and a capacity to make better use of feelings. Group members take roles such as 'doubling' (representing the alter-ego of the problem-presenter, speaking the unspoken thoughts and feelings) and 'auxiliary egos' (significant others) in the individual's psychodrama. Most groupworkers will not become psychodrama therapists, but the techniques offer much scope for creative adaptation in different forms of groupwork.

Sociodrama

Sociodrama (Jennings, 1973) works on similar principles to psychodrama, but the focus is on the social situation rather than the individual 'problem'. Thus an adolescent group may be asked to become an imaginary family facing some typical crisis, e.g. a fourteen-year-old girl staying out very late at night, and to dramatise it. Or they may re-enact an actual juvenile court or school classroom scene that some of them have experienced, each taking roles in the sociodrama. It is less personally threatening than psychodrama and offers an experiential approach to social learning. In all these drama techniques, the role of the leader at the warm-up stage is crucial in creating an atmosphere of trust and spontaneity. Drama therapy in a mixed programme can also energise members for other group activities.

Sculpting

This is another creative technique, also used in family therapy. People in a group are placed in a physical representation or 'sculpt' of their emotional relatedness, as seen by one member of that group. It can be used either to recreate an external group (family or other) to which one or more members belong, or to sculpt the group itself in the here-and-now. In a group sculpt, individuals may be able to show how they feel about themselves and the group in ways which they could not verbalise. When people are in position in a sculpt, they can be asked how they feel and how they would like it to be different. This can illustrate vividly how a move by one person has consequences for others, e.g. if A moves out of the scapegoat 'position', who will take his place? In sculpting, as with most experiential activities, it is essential to allow time for members to 'de-role' and discuss their experience. Strong feelings may be engendered which need to be worked through before the session ends.

Audio-visual aids

Video has various uses in groups, including skill development, fun and community action. There is no substitute for video for accurate direct feedback in social skills training, and portable video or sound equipment can be used by community and other groups to do interviews and make films relevant to their group and community goals. Video can be great fun, and also quite threatening, not to mention frustrating when it does not work properly! For all these reasons, its use in group programme requires care and planning. (Its use in groupwork training is discussed in Chapter 5.)

Indoor physical activities

Physical movement is a good facilitator in itself, quite apart from the direct skills and social learning which different kinds of games and indoor activities offer. There is scope for different levels of co-operation and sharing. Physical games are widely used in intermediate treatment with adolescents, but this type of activity also has an important place in adult groups. Dancing, yoga, bioenergetic exercises, or wrestling may form part of a group programme for adults, who tend to be more inhibited than children about physical interaction and movement. It is often helpful to the members if the leader demonstrates and participates, at least in the early stages.

Art and crafts

In social work groups this kind of creative activity is likely to be a therapeutic means to some less tangible end, e.g. drawing and painting may be the most effective means by which some members can communicate with others. For a detailed account of the potential of *art therapy* in groups see Liebmann (1986).

'Outside' activities

This refers to all those activities which necessitate the group moving away physically from its usual base. Included are trips, visits (educational/leisure), outdoor sports and pursuits, camping, community projects and many others. For some groups this will form the major part of their programme, for others it will be a minor but important part designed to provide diversity, perhaps an anticipated highlight, such as a boat trip, offering a new context for group experience. The effect can sometimes 'free-up' a group to move forward after a static period. There are practical problems to cope with such as transport, finance and insurance.

In groupwork, outside activities are usually of value in themselves, but they also are a means to some other goal which the group has. If the activity is, or becomes, the primary goal, then it may have a more appropriate place in educational, trade training or sports programmes.

Games and simulations

There are many games which groups can play as a different, and often very acceptable, way of interacting and learning. An example is a game designed to help members give each other personal feedback. One person volunteers to be the focus, and all the other group members have to think, silently, of an animal that the person particularly reminds them of. Then, in turn, each member divulges the chosen animal and gives reasons for the resemblance. This is both good fun and a relatively unthreatening way of giving personal feedback. Several comprehensive collections of group games are now available (see Brandes and Phillips, 1978; Brandes, 1982; Dearling and Armstrong, 1984; Ernst and Goodison, 1982).

Inter-group or inter-role activities

This refers to programmed contacts between a group and either other groups or individuals in particular roles. One example of an inter-group meeting that involved two FSU parents' groups has already been referred to (Walker, 1978). Bazalgette (1971) programmed groups for school-leavers and others in the 14–21 age-range, to meet individual adults who were in community roles carrying authority which had special significance for them, e.g. employer, vicar, policeman, social worker, careers advisory officer. Another group invited the leader of a youth club where some of them had been banned for unruly behaviour. A single parents' group invited a welfare-rights lawyer to discuss financial and legal problems. The aim of these interchanges may vary from social learning to role-testing to obtaining expert advice.

Interactions of this kind can be useful, especially in longer-term groups, but they can also be diversionary or even lead to disruptive competition and hostility. They need to be programmed with caution. The beginning groupworker sometimes experiences a self-generated pressure to involve outside 'experts' to compensate for feelings of personal inadequacy, or fears that the group will not have enough to do. These pressures need to be tested against the likelihood of positive gain. The early forming–storming stages of a new group are not usually a good time to bring in outside influences. These are likely to be coped with better when the group has developed its own strength and cohesion, and perhaps needs a new stimulus.

Relaxation exercises

Many groups, particularly those with members suffering from high levels of mental and/or physical stress, find it useful to include periods of time devoted to relaxation (one 'back-pain' group started each session with 20 minutes relaxation). Audio-tapes 'leading' relaxation sequences are widely available, and the straightforward method of tensing up and then relaxing all the different parts of the body in turn, is very effective.

Assignments or homework

These have already been referred to as those programme activities which an individual or sub-group agrees to carry out between sessions. The tasks need to be manageable, carrying a high expectation of 'success', and, if possible, be fairly specific and easily evaluated by the individual member or sub-group.

An example of effective use of group programme

The reader is referred to an excellent account by Ross and Bilson (1981) of the thoughtful and imaginative use of group programme. Their 'Sunshine Group' was a twelve session intensive group for children of both sexes, aged 9–11, who had experienced sexual assault either as perpetrator or victim. The workers carefully assessed the need to be met and worked out a flexible programme response which included a whole range of creative play, discussion, games and drama techniques, as well as a three-day residential period after the eighth session.

Some difficulties which can arise in groups and possible ways of resolving them

One of the main reasons for planning and preparing a group very carefully is to reduce the likelihood of serious dysfunctioning occurring, but groupwork is about people interacting together, often under stress, and this inevitably produces some difficulties as well as many benefits. Two of the most common causes of concern and anxiety for groupworkers and group members are, firstly, when individuals get into problematic roles, and secondly when the whole group takes on a stance which seems to get in the way of group development and task-achievement. We shall consider each of these in turn, developing a consistent conceptual framework, selecting a few of the most common examples of each 'problem', and suggesting various strategies which may help the worker, and the group, to resolve the difficulty.

The individual and the group

A group is a dynamic interacting system in which each individual's role and behaviour is in varying degrees a function of the group-as-a-whole and of group process as well as an individual characteristic. As a group develops, the roles get shared around among the members. Sometimes an individual finds a role which enables him both to contribute to, and to benefit from, the group in a way suiting his personal resources and needs. At other times people get 'stuck' in problematic roles which may be dysfunctional for them, and also for the group.

Examples of problematic roles are the 'scapegoat', the 'monopoliser', the 'silent member', the 'deviant', the 'absent member', and the 'disrupter'. In order to understand what is happening (and therefore to begin to have ideas about a solution) a group perspective is needed which, whilst appreciating that an individual often attracts a particular role, recognises that he can also have it reinforced or 'put on him' by others, often unconsciously. Thus, for example, scapegoating is a process in which one group member is isolated and has ascribed to him (negative) feelings, wishes or behaviour which others are unable to recognise or accept in themselves and then attack in the scapegoat. A monopoliser can only dominate a group as long as others tacitly allow him to do so, and a silent member may find himself in that position because others are not open to what he may have to contribute. The basic theoretical assumption is that individual behaviours may often have *group purpose* — they are functional, in a process sense, for the group, although they may be dysfunctional for task-achievement. This has implications for worker response and problem resolution.

We shall now consider a range of possible responses applicable to any problematic individual role behaviour in a group and then comment briefly on the special features of scapegoating, monopolising and being silent.

(1) *Do nothing*. It is essential that the worker waits a little while, firstly to tune-in to the dynamic and make sure she understands what is happening and secondly in the hope that group members may take some initiative themselves in drawing attention to, and helping to resolve the difficulty. To allow the problem to persist indefinitely, however, is to abdicate the responsibility that is part of being a group leader.

(2) *Indirect responses*. These are approaches in which the worker tries to influence what is happening without drawing attention to it explicitly or directly. One way of doing this which can be quite effective is to use group programme. This means using different group structures, activities or exercises to shift the group balance. One simple structure is 'going round the circle' in which each member has his turn to contribute without having to claim it by 'getting in'. (Many people find a role offered by a structure an easier basis for contributing in a group than when they have to take the risk and the initiative themselves.) Alternatively workers may use seating arrangements, non-verbal communication and various other forms of 'engineering' to reinforce desired changes and free up the problematic role.

(3) *Direct implicit responses*. Some responses can be direct without referring explicitly to the underlying issue. An example of this is making a point of offering a silent member the opportunity to speak, asking a monopoliser to keep quiet while somebody else is contributing, or

turning away from the monopoliser and saying 'what do others think?'.

(4) *Direct explicit responses*. There are three possibilities here, each making explicit reference to 'the problem': (a) *To speak directly to the individual* ('Mary, you seem to be getting blamed for everything that goes wrong in this group', 'Jim, can you tell the rest of us what makes it difficult for you to speak in this group', 'Jean, you talk so much it's difficult to hear the important things you have to say'); (b) *to speak directly to the rest of the group* ('I think we need to try and understand why you are always having a go at Mary', 'Does it concern the rest of you that Jim is silent and gets ignored', 'The rest of you are letting Jean do nearly all the talking in this group'); or (c) *to address the group-as-a-whole* ('I suggest we stop what we're doing for a few minutes because we're not working together very well as a group at the moment . . . I'm sure we've all noticed that . . . Let's try and find out what everyone in the group thinks about what's been happening and see if we can agree a way of working together which will be better for everyone . . .

Of these three 'explicit' options, the first two will, on occasion, be appropriate/necessary but they both have the basic flaw (as a starting point) of reinforcing the split between the individual and the group. The third option of addressing the group-as-a-whole is generally to be preferred because it reinforces the basic premise of shared responsibility for what happens in the group. It takes a bit of courage for the worker to be direct and explicit about the difficulty, and initially the intervention may be met by denial or hostility, but there is likely also to be considerable relief in the group that something everyone was aware of can now be talked about. The worker's aim is for a resolution which both frees the individual from the unhelpful role and enables the whole group to move forward with the task. This process often includes the facilitation of feedback between members about how they are experiencing each other's behaviour.

The worker herself is powerfully affected by the group dynamic and this can sometimes lead her to protect (the scapegoat, silent member) or attack (the monopoliser, the scapegoaters) which is unlikely to benefit the individual or the group except in extreme circumstances where, for example, the physical protection of an individual or the removal of a severe disrupter may be necessary. Consultation can be particularly effective in enabling a worker to disentangle her personal feelings sufficiently to facilitate productive change in the group.

(5) *Contact outside the group*. Another possible response is to make contact with the individual member outside the group. This approach

is to be used selectively and sensitively depending on (a) the urgency of the individual need and the availability or otherwise of alternative sources of support/contact, and (b) the extent to which the individual contact is likely to facilitate a group resolution of the problem. What is to be avoided is getting into a special relationship with one group member outside the group which includes discussion of their relationship with other members in the group. This is group business and needs to be resolved within the group.

The 'monopoliser'

The monopoliser may be useful to the group in the early stages of uncertainty and dependency but as time passes he becomes not only increasingly resented by other members, but also a threat to the position of the leader. It is nearly always necessary to take action with a persistent monopoliser because there can be serious repercussions among the other members who, if the worker does not take an initiative, may be deterred from returning to the group. The important thing to hold on to (as you struggle to manage your own strong feelings!) is that frequently beneath the monopoliser's stream of verbiage that person has something important to express and contribute to the group. Exceptionally a monopoliser may be so destructive that the last resort of exclusion from the group is necessary.

The 'scapegoat'

The scapegoat is unlikely or unwilling to defend himself effectively or to do much about it. This suggests that the role is in some way functional and satisfying for him as well as for the group. Negative attention may be preferred to no attention. Typically, groups ostracise, institutionalise or encapsulate scapegoats. The more institutionalised they become the harder it is to relinquish the role because it fits everyone's expectations. The worker often feels drawn to protect the scapegoat and to reverse the blame to the rest of the group, or particular 'persecutory' individuals. Even without this, the mere exposure of the scapegoating phenomenon in the group is often unpopular (because it faces others with *their* 'nasty bits') and it is not uncommon for the worker to get scapegoated instead − be prepared!

The 'silent member'

I personally find this one of the most difficult situations to know how to respond to helpfully. I think there are two reasons for this. The personal reason is that I rarely find myself in this position in small groups and therefore am not always as understanding or sensitive as I ought to be! The more general reason is that silent members do not intrude on group business and other members in such an obvious way, and it is sometimes difficult to judge why they are quiet and whether they wish to remain silent or to be helped to participate. A member may take on a silent role for a variety of reasons, such as fear of self-disclosure, lack of assertiveness, self-protection against vulnerability, fear of losing control, or to cope with a perceived threat from one or more others in the group. Experience suggests that people who are habitually quiet in groups would usually like to be helped to be more (verbally) active, but without being put on the spot.

Structured opportunities, or quiet encouragement are appreciated. Shulman (1984) suggests the worker speak to the quiet member outside the group and make a secret arrangement about signals in the group. As stated earlier, I think contact outside the group does have a place as another strategy in the resolution of these individual behaviours, particularly when it really does seem to be more an individual than a group problem, but in general I prefer in-group methods without special alliances or secrets between worker and member.

Shulman (1984) has a good section on this topic, and so do Yalom (1975) and Whitaker (1985). Garland and Kolodny (1972) and Anstey (1982) give special attention to scapegoating.

'Whole group' problems

Every groupworker will have experienced times when the whole group takes on a particular characteristic which appears to be impeding progress. The group may go silent, apathetic, resistant, attacking, depressed, jokey. The first thing, as worker, is to manage your own feelings about what is happening — there's usually an important message if you are able to listen and not just feel frustrated, angry, depressed or impotent. The range of possible responses is similar to that suggested above for problematic individual roles, but the focus of interest is much more likely to be the worker–group relationship and the issue of authority, particularly in the early stages of a group. Shulman (1984) has pointed out that the members have to deal with the worker's ability to control, to make demands and to care, as well as coping with her limitations and her role as 'outsider' in the group. A second area which may be contributing to group problems is intimacy and the relationship between members.

I never cease to be amazed at how different the mood of the same group can be from one session to the next, which indicates the wisdom of 'hanging in there' before reacting too swiftly. When the time does come to act, the response may be direct or indirect, implicit or explicit. As a general guideline, observation and comments on what is going on are more positively received than clever interpretations or apparent criticisms of the members. Explicit use of what you are feeling can be helpful, and risk-taking often produces positive results. For example, a group of offenders in an 'alcohol discussion group' were expected to share with the others their past drinking behaviour, in response to questioning in the 'hot seat'. Nobody volunteered and the atmosphere got very sticky. Ultimately one of the two workers agreed to take the hot-seat herself; the group's energy visibly returned and she was subjected to questioning firstly by her co-worker and then by other group-members. After a while a group-member volunteered to take the hot-seat and the impasse was broken. One potential trap in this resolution is the worker getting caught in a member role and being used vicariously by members, thus perpetuating risk-avoidance rather than role-modelling risk-taking in a way they then can follow. Having a co-worker can be most helpful in this type of situation because she can 'manage' the episode and hold on to the worker – member boundary, helping her colleague to do likewise.

For further discussion about the ways in which different kinds of group culture and structures develop, and ways in which workers can facilitate group development and 'enabling solutions' see Heap, 1985, Shulman, 1984 and Whitaker, 1985. Heap (Chapter 6) has a particularly useful section which explores the different reasons for 'group silences' and he suggests a range of different 'matched' responses by the worker.

Final comment on difficulties

When approaching individual and group difficulties it is always necessary to remember that some individuals can be very vulnerable in groups and are potential casualties (see Galinsky and Schopler, 1977). They may, for example, lose control of themselves, sob violently or behave in a way likely to damage themselves or others. They may become depressed and withdrawn. If their vulnerability is predominantly a personal matter, then maximum support should be offered to the individual within and outside the group. (In extreme cases they may need to withdraw from the group.) If, however, the vulnerability is a group-induced phenomenon of the kind discussed in this section, then it is group business to work it out together, with the aim of individuals owning their own agendas instead of depositing them on others.

5. Developing and Evaluating Groupwork Skills and Knowledge

This chapter considers firstly the basic *training* necessary for skilled groupwork practice, and then goes on to discuss *recording, consultation and evaluation*, all three of which are important elements in the development of effective groupwork programmes and group skills. The chapter and the book conclude with a qualitative evaluation by a group member of how he benefited from membership of a particular group.

Training

Groupwork training has several ingredients which will be considered here.

Experiential understanding of group membership

Whatever type of groupwork a social worker expects to practise, she needs to develop sensitive understanding of group processes and the role of group member. This is done primarily through experiencing and learning about her own feelings and behaviour as a group member in interaction with others. There are several ways of doing this; firstly, by participating in here-and-now groups which have the task of studying individual and group behaviour, as it happens. Groups of this kind are often described as 'training' or 'sensitivity' groups and include the T-group, Tavistock group and other models (Shaffer and Galinsky, 1974; Palmer, 1978). They vary in the emphasis placed upon authority, intimacy, relationships, stereotyping and the group as a system, but all include an intensive exploration of the feelings which people have about themselves and others in groups. This kind of training sensitises the practitioner to the irrational and unconscious forces which can influence group behaviour, and the task.

Secondly, there are existing work-groups, e.g. student seminar group, social work team or hostel staff group, which may include understanding of their own process as part of their programme. An external consultant is likely to be needed to help with this task. On some groupwork training courses, groups are created with a task blending conceptual and experiential understanding of group processes (Douglas, 1978b.).

Thirdly, opportunities may occur to work on personal problems and issues as a member of a therapeutic or problem-solving group, thus gaining first-hand experience of what it is like to seek help from others in a group. In some therapies, such as group analysis, transactional analysis, psychodrama and gestalt, substantial member experience is a required part of training and qualification. A modified version of this is the Shared Decision Making model developed by Maple (1977, Part III), in which a peer training group of five or six persons has one member 'presenting' a problem (professional or personal) which the others have to concentrate on helping them with, using a goal-oriented method.

A fourth approach uses games and simulation exercises. The most effective ones are those where the trainee is asked to participate in the exercise as authentically as possible *as herself*, as distinct from role playing. In exercises of this kind, with no prescribed roles, e.g. the island game (Brandes and Phillips, 1978) stranded in the desert (Johnson and Johnson, 1975), the Zin obelisk (Woodcock, 1979) or 'who should get the prize?', the roles which a trainee finds herself taking — particularly if there is an observed consistency across different groups and exercises — are likely to be significant indicators of her personal style in groups, as well as providing experience of the pressure which group members face when trying to find their 'place' in a new group.

Simulated experience of the group leader role

This is an essential stage which often gets omitted when practitioners are left to make the big leap from experiential group membership to designated leadership of a client group. The essence of this training is creating group and groupwork scenarios, either fictional or simulations of real groups, in which the trainee takes a leader or co-leader role. Video is used to film the simulation, which is then played back for critique, feedback and analysis. Leader skills and alternative approaches are practised and developed in this way. If video is not available, sound recordings can be used and also observers with specified briefs. The 'goldfish bowl' method of an outer circle observing an inner circle can be used with larger training groups. Simulations can also be devised to practise pre-group interviews, and the group preparation stage when the social worker has to negotiate with colleagues and management to obtain the resources necessary to support a group project. When using these methods, it is important that feedback is offered constructively.

Using the literature

Practitioners learn in different ways and will use books, articles and training manuals to suit their personal approach. Some will prefer to read about it first and then try it out in practice, whereas others seem to need to experience the issues first before they are motivated to delve into the literature. Relevant texts have been referred to throughout this book, and appear in the bibliography at the end.

Learning through observing and doing

The trainee can learn much from the experienced groupworker through observing her practice, either directly when working with a group, through training films (see, for example, the training video 'Developing your Groupwork Skills', Bristol University, 1986) or through written or spoken accounts of practice methods. It is essential, however, that the trainee develops her own style and skills at an early stage, and this means undertaking groupwork practice on training placements with skilled supervision. Experiences of both single and co-leadership should, if possible, be included in this formative stage. The associated skills of recording, use of consultation, and evaluation will now be discussed.

Recording

Groupwork recording is more difficult than recording one-to-one interviews because of the complex nature of a small group. In groups with a task-oriented focus, recording will be concerned with tangible tasks, plans, actions and decisions. In a person-oriented group, where feelings, relationships and non-verbal communication receive high priority, recording is dealing with intangibles, perhaps the most difficult of all to write about. Most groups records attempt to communicate both content and process.

Groupwork recording has several different purposes as follows:

Agency requirements

Most agencies require some written information on the official records about each piece of work done, particularly if it forms part of their statutory responsibilities. One difficulty is that records are usually designed for individual and family information, not group approaches. If the full group-record appears in each individual's file there are problems of confidentiality as well as the difficulty of picking out the sections which are relevant to that individual. An alternative is to keep a separate *group folder* and to record only brief individual information in the individual file, e.g. '17.11.86 John attended the group', or '17.11.86 Group meeting. John was involved in a fight when he arrived, but later showed real progress in co-operating with other boys to make a puppet stage.'

A confidentiality issue also arises when a group member is under the statutory supervision of a social worker not involved with the group. The group member (and the social worker) should know what kinds of information, if any, will be passed on to 'their' social worker, including what will be written down on their records. If a group folder approach is used, it raises interesting questions about where it is kept and to whom it belongs — the groupworker, the group, the agency . . . ?

Training and skill development

Detailed records, whether written or tape-recorded in sound or video, are a key element in any groupwork training programme. Apart from their direct value to the practitioner in clarifying thoughts and feelings about a session, they provide material which can be available to the trainer or consultant for supervision sessions.

Planning, evaluation and research

Some recording, however brief, of every group session or event facilitates assessment of individual and group progress, and programme planning. One of the main purposes is to have a record of changes over a period of time. This is often a surprise and encouragement to both the worker and group members themselves, who can easily underestimate the extent of progress over a period of months or even weeks. Systematic and planned recording is an essential part of any groupwork evaluation or research.

For direct use in work with members

Records do not have to be secret agency property and can be available to group members, or better still, written by the members themselves. A group record or diary may be kept, with different members taking responsibility for writing it up. The contents of the diary may be referred to and used as part of the programme. Alternatively, individual members can keep their own personal record. Group leaders can give written feedback on both group and individual records, using that medium as another way of communicating with members. A very simple individual record which has been used successfully and can be adapted to different groups is given below.

Name:	Group:	Date:
1.	Since the last group, what have you done, or what has happened that was important?	(To be completed before a session starts.)
2.	What are you hoping to achieve at this meeting?	
3.	What have you achieved at this meeting?	(To be completed at the end of the session.)
4.	How do you feel about it?	
5.	Groupworker's notes (feedback)	(To be added between sessions.)

(A section for peer feedback can be included if acceptable on confidentiality grounds.)

Written records

The three media for recording are audiotape, videotape and written records. The group's permission is essential for the first two, with a clear understanding about who, if anyone, will have access to the tapes. This is made much easier if the tape is used subsequently in the group, so the members are involved with it rather than feeling something is being done to them, or taken away from them. Tapes are very useful for supervision purposes but also very time consuming. As most groups have to rely on the written record, this is now considered in more detail.

Written records are not normally made during a group session, except when particular decisions need to be noted, perhaps about future programme plans. Unless the members are involved in the recording, the leader(s) will write it up afterwards. Co-leaders can pre-arrange that one of them will be responsible, usually the one with the more secondary role in that session, though it doesn't always work out that way! It is important to make some brief notes *as soon as possible* after the session. As time passes, memory distorts and omits. The full version needs to have some structure to it, including scope for content and process.

In therapeutic/talking groups the clock or interaction chronogram (Cox, 1973) is sometimes used. This consists of a clock face with a circle for each participant, each circle being divided into three segments (see Fig. 5.1). Significant behaviour or achievement is written into each segment for each member. Arrows between members can be used to indicate the directions and quality of interactions.

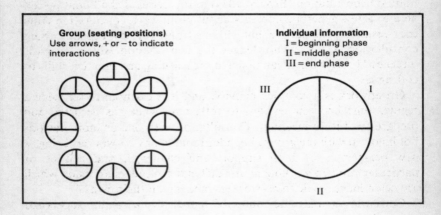

Fig. 5.1

A written outline, adaptable for most groups, to be completed by the leader or a designated member, can be made under the following headings.

1. Basic data to include date, venue, number of meeting, members and leaders present/absent. (In a sedentary group, a clock-type map indicating seating positions can be useful.)
2. Plan for the session, as decided beforehand (perhaps referring to the group as a whole, individual members, leaders).
3. Content, themes, activities, decisions (task emphasis).

4. Process, group interactions (relationship emphasis).
5. Individuals. Notes on each member's participation and progress.
6. Leaders. Notes on leader/co-leader functioning.
7. Summary, linking what happened to aims and future plans.

The difficult sections are 3 and 4 which attempt to communicate what actually happened in the group. The type of group and its aims, and the practitioner's own style are likely to determine how the group is recorded. In the early stages more detail is needed, but at later stages it is changes and significant events which are particularly worth noting.

Consultation and supervision

These are major topics in their own right and readers interested in exploring the skills of consultation in more depth are referred to my book on consultation (Brown, 1984) in this series. I shall limit myself here to a few general comments about groupwork consultation from the consultee's perspective, but within a framework for thinking about consultation which acknowledges the contribution which even the 'greenest' groupworker can make to the learning and practice-skills of colleagues.

Groupwork is a complex activity, and it is essential to set aside a regular time between sessions to reflect on what has occurred and prepare for future meetings. Consultation with one or more persons not involved with the group, i.e. additional to any co-worker, brings a new perspective of both support and challenge, and can be of particular value in working at any difficult co-leadership issues which are often inaccessible to co-workers meeting on their own.

Consultation may be obtained either from one's supervisor (accessible as of right, but with the power differential which may inhibit free exchange) or from elsewhere (which requires close liaison with the supervisor who probably holds agency accountability for the group and its activities).

Both the source and type of consultation need careful thought. The source may be intra-team, from elsewhere in the agency, or from 'outside'. The type may be *tutorial* (1−1 between expert/senior and novice/junior) *tandem or co-counselling* (1−1 between 'equals' on a reciprocal basis) or *group* (a group meeting of groupworker peers, with or without a facilitator). When there is co-leadership it is essential that both workers participate in the same consultation, so that 1−1 models are actually 1−2.

When able to choose, the groupworker needs to think carefully about what kind of consultation arrangements to negotiate, bearing in mind the need for trust without cosiness! Whatever the arrangements, an explicit agreement about the terms and aims of consultation is needed at the beginning, which should, if possible, be at an early stage of the pre-group phase so that consultation help can be available when crucial preparation and planning decisions are being taken.

Group models of consultation can be particularly effective when the participants are working with broadly similar types of groups, so that learning continues when other people's groups are being discussed. A facilitator is needed most when the peer group is composed of inexperienced workers. Group composition criteria apply as much to social worker groups as to client groups! A key decision is whether consultancy takes place within the normal team supervision arrangements, or outside the team structure. In teams where there is much mutual support and professional sharing, where the team leader has groupwork supervision skills, and where most team members get involved in groupwork, there is a firm basis for group-supervision in the team. Yet even in such a promising setting, an outside consultant can have an important role in confirming and challenging team assumptions and practice.

In groupwork consultation/supervision there is a wide range of potential *focus*, and misunderstandings sometimes arise when consultant and consultee have different ideas about what is appropriate. The range of focus extends from (a) the workers (each individually, and the co-working relationship), (b) the dynamics of the group as-a-whole, (c) individual members, (d) group programme and activities, (e) external factors such as the agency, institutional, community or family contexts of the participants.

Traditionally groupwork (and indeed social work) consultation has relied on the workers' reports on what has happened. Sometimes direct information such as audio or videotape recordings is available, but the concept of live consultation (Kingston and Smith, 1983), now often regarded as integral to work with family groups, has not yet attracted serious interest as a suitable method for groupwork consultation.

Evaluation

Evaluation of groupwork can be undertaken both formally and informally. It may be concerned with assessing the effectiveness of a particular group method of intervention and/or with monitoring the contribution group participation has made to the achievement of each individual member's identified goals. The more formal type of evaluative groupwork research is relatively rare in the UK (but see Smith *et al.*, 1972; Caddick and Brown, 1982), and readers who are interested in the methodological issues are referred to Caddick (1983) and Dies (1978). Whitaker (1985, Chapter 6) demonstrates how 'by relatively little additional pre-planning and later work, the ordinary task of informal monitoring and assessment can be transformed into small-scale formal research'. What we are concerned with here is the responsibility which every practitioner has, in collaboration with her clients, to engage in regular evaluative efforts to try and find out what the social work intervention is achieving (outcome) and how it is being experienced (process).

Evaluation of the effectiveness of a group is an essential part of the ending phase, but it should also be a recurrent theme during the group's life as worker and clients review progress, and if necessary redefine goals and methods. Groupwork evaluation is complicated by the number of people involved, each with personal agendas. In many formed groups the progress of each individual is what counts, and the group approach is best assessed by the impact it has for each member. If, say, in a group of ten members, five achieve their goals, but five fail to achieve theirs, statements can be made about the effectiveness or otherwise of that group for each individual, but not so clearly over all. In a natural group, evaluation may be most significant at the group level if the goals are pitched at that level, e.g. 'to improve family members' communication with each other'. In a community group, evaluation could be in terms of some community change objective, such as the establishment of children's play facilities.

At whatever level evaluation is being used, it can only be meaningful if there has been some initial agreement or contract about goals and the means of trying to achieve them. The more specific the goals, the easier it will be to assess whether they have been achieved. This is not necessarily an argument for choosing very specific goals such as 'to hit my child not more than twice a week instead of every day', if less tangible goals like 'to feel more loving to my child' are needed. There is a balance to be struck between behaviourally specific and qualitatively significant goals.

Example: A support group for lone fathers with the general group aim of sharing experiences and ideas relating to managing a family single-handed.Within this general aim, more specific aims were identified as: developing a social life; caring for and controlling your children; discussing relationships with women and remarriage; sorting out money problems.

Each of these aims was different for each group member and had to be defined individually, e.g. for Fred 'to go out socially at least once every week' (easy to measure), or for Jim 'to cope better with my sixteen-year-old daughter's rebellious attitude' (less tangible and so more difficult to measure). More specific behaviours, e.g. 'to talk to her for half an hour without losing my temper' are possible but may over-simplify.

Having clarified *what* the goals are for each individual (and they may be changed or added to as the group develops and new needs emerge), the next question is *how* to assess whether the goals have been reached. This can be done by the individual, the group or the leader, or all three. It is important that some part of the evaluation (of self, peers and the worker(s)) is written down as well as shared verbally in the group, because group pressures may inhibit individual statements. In addition to written and verbal evaluation at the end, written feedback can also be obtained several weeks or months after the group is over, when members may have a better perspective on the experience and know whether any desired changes have been sustained. This can be done by sending each member a simple follow-up questionnaire (an s.a.e. improves the return rate!) or using structured follow-up interviews, with both general questions about the group:

Example: Before you came to the group, what did you expect it to be like? If you found it different, in what ways was it different? Did you find the group very helpful/helpful/neutral/unhelpful/very unhelpful?

and also more specific questions:

Example: If you found the group helpful, can you say in what way it (a) helped you personally, (b) helped other group members? If you found the group unhelpful, can you say why?

Objective evaluation of groupwork effectiveness is difficult to obtain because of the complexity of the variables and problems of accurate measurement. This should not deter the groupworker from rough-and-ready methods, which obtain some useful information for future planning and agency policy. An awareness that you are expected to evaluate outcome makes you more likely to think carefully with members at the beginning of a group about what they hope to achieve, and to set realistic attainable goals. The use of a personal record for each member, as described above, is a useful method of continuous evaluation.

I would like to conclude with a written account by a lone father of his experience in a lone fathers' group. It is not based on a set question-naire or evaluation of specific goals, but is a moving account of what that group achieved for that person and others, as he experienced it.

A group member's experience

'I joined the group only three months after becoming a single parent. In the space of literally a few weeks I had changed from being a reasonably happily married man to a wounded and confused single man with a small child to care for. My first concern was that the trauma for my son be minimised and so I gave up completely all efforts to work in order to maintain for him a settled and orderly home-life.

'Thus, when I joined the group it was as a man who unexpectedly had lost wife, lover, my son's mother, and career. The poignancy of this situation was highlighted in one fairly small aspect. In my work in caring for the mentally handicapped I had to handle supplementary benefit books for eight people and every Monday morning signed and cashed about eight coupons for other people. Suddenly I was signing one for myself.

'Only those who have experienced it can understand the whirlwind of feelings that seem to overpower one completely at such times: rage, jealousy, longing, frustration, humiliation, loneliness, bitterness, fear, worry, all taking over from one another in a seemingly endless kaleidoscope. But the group helped: others had been there and others were still going through the same.

'From the first week one felt less alone. We exchanged household hints, where to get the cheapest children's clothes, how to save on fuel, how to save on food. I received tips on how to get a little bit more from the DHSS and rebates on electricity. For me this concentration on the practical and domestic helped to keep my feet rooted in each day.

'Other group members had to cope with far greater difficulties than I did and this put my problems into clear perspective. I had a good flat. I had no disputes over property or custody. I had one amiable son whom I have been very close to since the day he was born. Others had problems that were monumental in comparison. One man had three children, one of whom was epileptic. Another had teenage daughters who completely baffled him. Another had spent his whole life rearing five children in cramped conditions.

'Some were a year or more past the worst of their crisis and could observe in us beginners patterns of thought and feeling they had experienced. This was a great comfort, to know that the violence of one's feelings would come and go but would eventually settle down.

'A major topic of discussion, and one returned to again and again, was of course children. Here I was far more confident as the rearing of my child was and is something that fits easily on my shoulders and so in this area I felt able to give something back to the group. One major fear, of course, and I think this was especially mine, was that our children would grow up with a distorted view of women. I found no answer to this worry. A lasting impression from these discussions was that this was the most important factor for consideration. Anyone who thinks men cannot, because they are men, bring up children and all the problems they bring and find fulfilment in the experience, would have been enlightened if they had heard these conversations.

'As is to be expected, there was much discussion of women and this was at times quite naturally very distorted. Some of the group tried to balance this by keeping in mind that their experience of women was not to be projected on to all women. Others were immovably of the opinion that all women were feckless, lazy, completely unable to bear responsibility and that marriage was a waste of effort. These discussions were important. I was attracted to women. I had been deeply wounded by a woman and so in a turmoil of attraction and defensive rejection, I was then going rapidly from woman to woman perhaps out of loneliness, perhaps out of revenge, probably both. So it was important to me to bring out into the open my feelings lest this destructive pattern go on endlessly.

'Some members of the group felt we should meet and talk with single mothers. Some of us disagreed and I still do, although perhaps now I would reserve that opinion for those who are recently single and in a highly emotional state. It would be quite helpful, I am sure, to talk with women as single parents and householders when we were adjusted to that status. But to be in a mixed group at a time when we were still wounded lovers would have great dangers, I think, for many of our feelings about the opposite sex were very confused. I found the exclusive company of men in this group of great comfort. I think now, after a year has passed, a mixed group would not hold dangers.

'When I first went to the group I decided beforehand that if I were going to spend the evening amongst a roomful of moaning, self-pitying men, I would only attend once. Nothing impressed me more than our determination to stay afloat and maintain our self-respect. This was, I think, why some of us had no wish to carry on with the group more than the seven weeks. Our status as fathers alone could become our identity and the centre of our approach to life.

'For myself, I have now no wish to make special formal contact with other single parents, but in the midst of my crisis months, the support and help of this group was invaluable and so if at any time my experience could help others, I would be only too glad to participate again.'

(I would like to thank the former group member for this generous contribution. He prefers to remain anonymous.)

Bibliography

Note: The Bibliography includes all the references made in the book. A selection of these have been asterisked (*). They are basic texts and articles which between them offer the reader a comprehensive foundation in groupwork theory and skills. (About half of those asterisked are published in the UK.)
SWG refers to the journal *Social Work with Groups*

Alissi, A. and Casper, M. (eds, 1985), '*Time as a Factor in Groupwork*: Time-Limited Group Experiences', *SWG* 8(2) (New York, Haworth Press).

Anstey, M. (1982) 'Scapegoating in Groups: some Theoretical Perspectives and a Case Record of Intervention', *SWG* 5(3).

Aplin, G. (1977) 'Some Thoughts in Teaching the Design and Evaluation of Groupwork Practice' in N. McCaughan and K. McDougall (eds), *Group Work – A guide for Teachers and Practitioners*, NISW Paper No. 7.

Bales, R. F. (1950), *Interaction Process Analysis* (Reading, Mass., Addison-Wesley).

Bazalgette, J. (1971), *Freedom, Authority and the Young Adult* (London, Pitman).

Bernstein, S. (1972), 'Values and Group Work' in S. Bernstein (ed.), *Further Explorations in Group Work* (London, Bookstall Publications).

*Bertcher, H. J. and Maple, F. F. (1977), *Creating Groups* (London, Sage Publications).

Blatner, H. A. (1973), *Acting-In: Practical Applications of Psychodramatic Methods* (Springer Publishing Company, Inc).

Bond, T. (1986), *Games for Social and Life Skills* (London, Hutchinson).

Brandes, D. (1982), *Gamesters 2* (London, Hutchinson).

*Brandes, D. and Phillips, H., (1978) *Gamesters' Handbook* (London, Hutchinson).

Breton, M. (1985), 'Reaching and Engaging People: Issues and Practice Principles', *SWG* 8(3).

*Brimelow, M. and Wilson, J. (1982), 'A Problem Shared', 'Drawing the Circle', 'Ourselves Alone', *Social Work Today*, 13 (19, 20, 21).

Briscoe, C. (1978), 'Programme Activities in Social Group Work', in N. McCaughan (ed.), *Group Work: Learning and Practice* (London, George Allen & Unwin).

*Bristol University (1986), *Developing your Groupwork Skills*, Skills Training Videotape (97 mins).

Brown, A. (1984), *Consultation* (London, Heinemann).

*Brown, A., Caddick, B., Gardiner, M. and Sleaman, S. (1982), 'Towards a British Model of Groupwork', *British Journal of Social Work*, 12(6) 587–605.

*Brown, A. and Seymour, B. (eds, 1983), *Intake Groups for Clients: a Probation Innovation*, SAUS (University of Bristol).

*Button, L. (1974) *Developmental Group Work with Adolescents* (University of London Press).

Caddick, B. (1983), 'Intake Group Evaluation' in A. Brown and B. Seymour (eds), *Intake Groups for Clients*, SAUS (University of Bristol).

Caddick, B., and Brown, A. (1982), 'The Problems and Promise of Evaluating Practice – a Groupwork Example' *Probation,* December 1982.

Cartwright, D. and Zander, A. (eds, 1968), *Group Dynamics: Research and Theory*, 3rd ed. (New York, Harper & Row).

Clough, R. (1982), *Residential Work* (Basingstoke, Macmillan).

Cooper, J. (1980), *Social Groupwork with Elderly People in Hospital* (Stoke on Trent, Beth Johnson Foundation).

Cox, M. (1973), 'The Group Therapy Interaction Chronogram', *British Journal of Social Work*, 3, (2).

Cressey, D. R. (1955), 'Changing Criminals: The Application of the Theory of Differential Association', *American Journal of Sociology*, 6 Sept. 1955.

Croxton, T. A. (1974), 'The Therapeutic Contract in Social Treatment' in P. Glasser, R. Sarri and R. Vinter (eds), *Individual Change Through Small Groups* (New York, The Free Press).

*Davies, B. (1975), *The Use of Groups in Social Work Practice* (London, Routledge & Kegan Paul).

Davis, L. (1980), 'Racial Balance – A Psychological Issue', *SWG* 3(2).

*Davis, L. (1984), 'Essential Components of Group Work with Black Americans', *SWG* 7(3).

*Dearling, A. and Armstrong, H. (1984 edn), *The Youth Games Book* (Renfrewshire, I. T. Resource Centre).

Derricourt, N. and Penrose, J. (1984), 'Groupwork with Young Offenders: Working out a theory for practice', *Social Work Education*, 4 (1).

Dies, R. R. (ed., 1978), 'Symposium on Therapy and Encounter Group Research', *Small Group Behaviour*, 9, (2).

Dies, R. R. and Cohen (1976) 'Content Considerations in Group Therapist Disclosure', *International Journal of Group Psychotherapy*.

Douglas T. (1970), *A Decade of Small Group Theory, 1960–70* (London, Bookstall Publications).

*Douglas, T. (1976), *Groupwork Practice* (London, Tavistock Publications).

*Douglas, T. (1978a), *Basic Groupwork* (London, Tavistock Publications).

Douglas, T. (1978b), 'A model for Teaching Group Work' in N. McCaughan (ed.), *Group Work: Learning and Practice* (London, George Allen & Unwin).

Douglas, T. (1983), *Groups* (London, Tavistock Publications).

*Ernst, S. and Goodison, L. (1982), *In our own hands: a book of Self-Help Therapy* (London, The Women's Press).

Fiedler, F. E. (1967), *A Theory of Leadership Effectiveness* (New York, McGraw-Hill).

French, J. R. P. and Raven, B. (1967), '*The Bases of Social Power*' in D. Cartwright (ed.), *Studies in Social Power* (Ann Arbor, Mich., Institute for Social Research).

*Galinsky, M. J. and Schopler, J. H. (1977), 'Warning: Groups May Be Dangerous', *Social Work*, March 1977.

Galinsky, M. and Schopler, J. H. (1980), 'Structuring Co-Leadership in Social Work Training', *SWG* 3(4).

*Galinsky, M. and Schopler, J. H. (1985), 'Patterns of Entry and Exit in Open-Ended Groups', *SWG* 8(2).

Garland, J. A., Jones, H. E. and Kolodny, R. L. (1965), 'A Model for Stages of Development in Social Work Groups' in S. Bernstein (ed.), *Explorations in Group Work* (Boston University School of Social Work).

*Garland, J. A. and Kolodny, R. L. (1972), 'Characteristics and Resolution of Scapegoating', in S. Bernstein (ed.), *Further Explorations in Groupwork* (London, Bookstall Publications).

*Garvin, C. (1981), *Contemporary Groupwork* (Englewood Cliffs, N. J., Prentice-Hall).

Garvin, C. (1974), 'Group Process: Usage and Uses in Social Work Practice', in P. Glasser, R. Sarri and R. Vinter, *Individual Change in Small Groups* (New York, The Free Press).

Garvin, C., Reid, W. and Epstein, L. (1976), 'A Task-Centred Approach' in Roberts, R. and Northen, H. (eds), *Theories of Social Work with Groups* (New York, Columbia U.P.).

*Glasser, P., Sarri, R. and Vinter, R. (eds, 1974), *Individual Change Through Small Groups* (New York, The Free Press).

Glasser, W. (1965), *Reality Therapy* (New York, Harper & Row).

Gorrell-Barnes, G. (1984), *Working with Families* (Basingstoke, Macmillan).

Greenberg, I. A. (1974), *Psychodrama: Theory and Therapy* (London, Souvenir Press).

Hall, E. T. (1969), *The Hidden Dimension* (New York, Doubleday).

Hankinson, I. and Stephens, D. (1985), 'In and out of Context', *Community Care* 4.7.85.

Hare, A. P. (1962), *Handbook of Small Group Research* (New York, The Free Press).

*Hartford, M. (1971), *Groups in Social Work* (New York, Columbia U.P.).

Heap, K. (1977), *Group Theory for Social Workers* (Oxford, Pergamon).

*Heap, K. (1979), *Process and Action in Work with Groups* (Oxford, Pergamon).

*Heap, K. (1985), *The Practice of Social Work with Groups* (London, George Allen & Unwin).

*Hodge, J. (1977), 'Social Groupwork: rules for establishing the Group', *Social Work Today*, 8(17) 1.2.77.

*Hodge, J. (1985), '*Planning for Co-Leadership*', Grapevine, 43, Fern Ave., Newcastle-Upon-Tyne, NE2 2QU.

Jennings, S. (1973), *Remedial Drama* (London, Pitman).

*Johnson, D. W. and Johnson, F. P. (1975), *Joining Together: Group Theory and Group Skills* (Englewood Cliffs, N.J., Prentice-Hall).

Jones, M. (1953), *The Therapeutic Community* (New York, Basic Books).

Jones, R. and Kerslake, A. (1979), *Intermediate Treatment and Social Work*, Community Care Practice Handbooks, 3. (London: Heinemann Educational Books).

Kesey, K. (1973), *One Flew Over the Cuckoo's Nest* (London, Pan Books, Picador).

Kingston, P. and Smith, D. (1983), 'Preparation for Live Consultation and Live Supervision', *Journal of Family Therapy*, 5, 219–233.

Konopka, G. (1963), *Social Groupwork: A Helping Process* (Englewood Cliffs, N.J., Prentice-Hall).

Laming, H. and Sturton, S. (1978), 'Group Work in a Social Services Department' in N. McCaughan (ed.), *Group Work: Learning and Practice* (London, George Allen & Unwin).

Lang, N. (1972), 'A Broad-Range Model of Practice in the Social Work Group', *Social Service Review*, 46, 76–89.

Lennox, D. (1982), *Residential Group Therapy for Children* (London, Tavistock Publications).

*Lieberman, M. A., Yalom, I. D. and Miles, M. B. (1973), *Encounter Groups: First Facts* (New York, Basic Books).

Liebmann, M. (1986), *Art Therapy for Groups* (Beckenham, Croom Helm).

Lippitt, R. and White, R. K. (1953), 'Leader Behaviour and Member Reaction in Three Different Climates' in D. Cartwright and A. Zander (eds, 1968), *Group Dynamics*, 3rd ed. (New York, Harper & Row).

Lindenfield, G. and Adams, R. (1984), *Problem-Solving through Self-Help Groups*, Ilkley, Self-Help Associates.

McCaughan, N. (1977), 'Group Behaviour: Some Theories for Practice' in C. Briscoe and D. N. Thomas (eds), *Community Work: Learning and Supervision* (London, George Allen & Unwin).

*McCaughan, N. (ed., 1978), *Groupwork: Learning and Practice* (London, George Allen & Unwin).

McCaughan, N. (1985), 'Groupwork going great guns', *Social Work Today*, 22.7.85.

McGuire, J. and Priestley, P. (1981), *Life After School* (Oxford, Pergamon).

Manor, O. (1986), 'The Preliminary Interview in Social Groupwork: Finding the Spiral Steps', *SWG* 9(2).

Maple, F. F. (1977), *Shared Decision Making* (London, Sage Publications).

Middleman, R. (1980), 'The Use of Program-Review and Update,' *SWG* 3(3).

Mounsey, N. (1983), 'It's not what you do, it's the way you do it', *Community Care*, 20.10.83.

*Mullender, A. and Ward, D. (1985), Towards an Alternative Model of Social Groupwork, *British Journal of Social Work*, 15(2).

Palmer, B. (1978), 'Fantasy and Reality in Group Life: a Model for Learning by Experience' in N. McCaughan (ed.), *Group Work: Learning and Practice* (London, George Allen & Unwin).

Palmer, T. B. (1973), 'Matching Worker and Client in Corrections', *Social Work*, 18, (2).

*Papell, C. P. and Rothman, B. (1966), 'Social Groupwork Models: Possession and Heritage', *Journal for Education for Social Work*, 2, (2) pp. 66–77. Reprinted in H. Specht and A. Vickery (eds, 1977), *Integrated Social Work Methods* (London, George Allen & Unwin).

*Papell, C. and Rothman, B. (1980), 'Relating the Mainstream Model of Social Work with Groups to Group Psychotherapy and the Structured Group Approach', *SWG* 3(2).

Parloff, M. and Dies, R. (1977), 'Group Psychotherapy Outcome Research, 1966–75', *International Journal of Group Psychotherapy*, July 1977.

Paulson, I., Burroughs, J. C. and Gelb, C. B. (1976), 'Co-therapy: What is the Crux of the Relationship', *The International Journal of Group Psychotherapy*, 1976.

Payne, C. (1978), 'Working with Groups in the Residential Setting' in N. McCaughan (ed.), *Group Work: Learning and Practice* (London, George Allen & Unwin).

Perls, F. (1971), *Gestalt Therapy Verbatim* (New York, Bantam Books).

Pirsig, R. M. (1976), *Zen and the Art of Motor-Cycle Maintenance* (New York, Corgi).

Pitman, E. (1984), *Transactional Analysis for Social Workers and Counsellors*, (London, Routledge and Kegan Paul).

*Priestley, P., McGuire, J. *et al.* (1978), *Social Skills and Personal Problem Solving* (London, Tavistock).

Reddin, W. J. (1970), *Managerial Effectiveness* (New York, McGraw-Hill).

Redl, F. (1951), 'Art of Group Composition' in S. Shulze (ed.), *Creative Living in a Children's Institution* (New York, Association Press).

*Reed, B. G. and Garvin, C. (eds, 1983), *Groupwork with Women/Groupwork with Men*, *SWG* 6(3/4) (Haworth Press).

Resnick, H. and Patti, R. (eds, 1980), *Change from Within* (Philadelphia, Temple University Press).

*Roberts, R. W. and Northen, H. (eds, 1976), *Theories of Social Work with Groups* (New York, Columbia U.P.).

Roman, M. (1976), 'Symposium: Family Therapy and Group Therapy – Similarities and Differences', *International Journal of Group Psychotherapy*, 1976.

*Rose, S. (1978), *Group Therapy: A Behavioural Approach* (Englewood Cliffs, N.J., Prentice-Hall).

Rose, S. (ed., 1980), *A Casebook in Group Therapy* (Englewood Cliffs, N.J., Prentice-Hall).

*Ross, S. and Bilson, A. (1981), 'The Sunshine Group: an Example of Social Work Intervention through the use of a Group', *SWG* 4 (1/2).

Sarri, R. and Galinsky, M. J. (1974), 'A Conceptual Framework for Group Development' in P. Glasser, R. Sarri and R. Vinter (eds, 1974), *Individual Change Through Small Groups* (New York, The Free Press).

Schopler, J. H. and Galinsky, M. (1984), 'Meeting Practice Needs: Conceptualizing the Open-Ended Group', *SWG* 7 (2).

Schutz, W. C. (1958), *FIRO: A Three-Dimensional Theory of Interpersonal Behaviour* (New York, Rinehart).

*Schwartz, W. (1971), 'On the Use of Groups in Social Work Practice' in W. Schwartz and S. R. Zalba, *The Practice of Group Work* (New York, Columbia U.P.).

*Shaffer, J. B. P. and Galinsky, M. D. (1974), *Models of Group Therapy and Sensitivity Training* (Englewood Cliffs, N.J., Prentice-Hall).

*Shaw, M. E. (1976), *Group Dynamics* (New York, McGraw-Hill).

Sherif, M. and Sherif, C. W. (1969), *Social Psychology* (New York, Harper & Row).

Shulman, L. (1978), 'A Study of Practice Skills', *Social Work*, 23(4).

*Shulman, L. (1984 edn), *The Skills of Helping: Individuals and Groups* (F. E. Peacock).

Silverman, P. (1980):, *Mutual Help Groups* (London, Sage).

Slater, P. E. (1958), 'Contrasting Correlates by Group Size', *Sociometry*, XXI, pp. 129–39.

Slavson, S. R. (1943), *An Introduction to Group Therapy* (New York, International Universities Press, Inc.)

Smith, C. S., Farrant, M. R. and Marchant, H. J. (1972), *The Wincroft Youth Project* (London, Tavistock).

Smith, P. B. (1978), 'Group Work as a Process of Social Influence' in N. McCaughan (ed.), *Group Work: Learning and Practice* (London, George Allen & Unwin).

*Smith, P. (1980), *Group Processes and Personal Change* (New York, Harper & Row).

Smith, P. (1985), 'Group Process Methods of Intervention in Race Relations' in J. Shaw, P. G. Noordlie *et al.* (eds), *Strategies for improving Race Relations* (Manchester University Press).

Stephenson, R. M. and Scarpitti, F. R. (1974), *Group Interaction as Therapy* (U.S.A., Greenwood Press).

Stevenson, O., Parsloe, P. *et al.* (1978), *Social Service Teams: The Practitioner's View* (London, HMSO for the DHSS).

Stodgill, R. M. (1948), 'Personal Factors Associated with Leadership: A Survey of the Literature', *Journal of Psychology*, 25, 35–71.

Thomas, D. N. (1978), 'Journey into the Acting Community: Experiences of Learning and Change in Community Groups' in N. McCaughan (ed.), *Group Work: Learning and Practice* (London, George Allen & Unwin).

Thomas, E. J. (1967), 'Themes in Small Group Theory' in E. J. Thomas (ed.), *Behavioural Science for Social Workers* (New York, The Free Press).

Todd, T. and Barcome, J. (1980), 'Use of Groups at Intake: Impact upon Clients, Staff and Program', *SWG* 3(3).

Treacher, A. and Carpenter, J. (eds, 1984), *Using Family Therapy* (Oxford, Basil Blackwell).

Truax, C. and Carkhuff, R. (1967), *Toward Effective Counselling and Psychotherapy: Training and Practice* (Chicago, Aldine).

*Tuckman, B. W. (1965), 'Developmental Sequence in Small Groups', *Psychological Bulletin*, 63(6).

Vinter, R., (1974), 'Program Activities: An Analysis of their Effects on Participant Behaviour', in P. Glasser, R. Sarri and R. Vinter (eds). *Individual Change Through Small Groups* (New York, The Free Press).

Vorrath, H. H. and Brendtro. L. K. (1984 edn.), *Positive Peer Culture* (Chicago, Aldine).

Walker, L. (1978), 'Work with a Parents Group' in N. McCaughan (ed.), *Group Work: Learning and Practice* (London, George Allen & Unwin).

Watson, D. (ed., 1985), *A Code of Ethics for Social Work* (London, Routledge and Kegan Paul).

*Wayne, J. and Avery, N. C. (1980), *Child Abuse: Prevention and Treatment Through Social Groupwork* (Boston, Charles Rivers Books).

*Whitaker, D. S. (1976), 'Some Conditions for Effective Work with Groups', *British Journal of Social Work*, 5, (4) 423–39.

*Whitaker, D. S. (1985), *Using Groups to Help People* (London, Routledge and Kegan Paul.

Woodcock, M. (1979), *Team Development Manual* (Aldershot, Gower).

*Yalom, I. D. (1975), *The Theory and Practice of Group Psychotherapy* (New York, Basic Books).

Ziller, R. (1965), 'Toward a Theory of Open and Closed Groups', *Psychological Bulletin*, LXIII.

Special issues of *Social Work with Groups* (= SWG above).

Vol. 3(4), 1980 *Co-Leadership in Social Work with Groups.*
Vol. 4(1), 1981, *Groupwork in Great Britain.*
Vol. 5(1), 1982, *Social Groupwork and Alcoholism.*
Vol. 5(2), 1982, *Groupwork with the Frail Elderly.*
Vol. 5(4), 1982, *The Use of Group Services in Permanency Planning for Children.*
Vol. 6(1), 1983, *Activities and Action in Groupwork.*
Vol. 6(3/4), 1983, *Groupwork with Women/Groupwork with Men.*
Vol. 7(3), 1984, *Ethnicity in Social Group Work Practice.*
Vol. 7(4), 1984, *Groupwork with Children and Adolescents.*
Vol. 8(2), 1985, *Time as a Factor in Groupwork.*

Author Index

Subject Index